# A HEAD FOR BUSINESS

*A*

# HEAD

*FOR*

# BUSINESS

## HOW BRITAIN'S TOP BUSINESS LEADERS
## CONTINUE TO SUCCEED

## CORINNE SIMCOCK

KOGAN
PAGE

First published in 1992

Kogan Page Limited
120 Pentonville Road
London   N1 9JN

**British Library Cataloguing in Publication Data**
A CIP record for this book is available from the British Library.

ISBN 0 7494 0608 9

Typeset by J&L Compostion Ltd, Filey, North Yorkshire
Printed in England by Clays Ltd, St Ives, plc

# Contents

# Acknowledgements

With grateful thanks to each of the participants, especially to Peter Gummer for his spectacular efforts on my behalf. My thanks also to Carolyn Lambert, Paul Godfrey, Robin Turner and all at the Westminster Boating Base.

# Introduction

*Successful management is an art form, not a science. People who try to reduce it to a science do not succeed*
*Christopher Lewinton, Chairman, TI Group.*

Managing through a recession is indeed a challenging task. Undoubtedly there are a lot of lessons to be learned which can help businesses not only to prosper when the economy starts to pick up again, but also to avoid being caught by the next downturn.

In *A Head For Business*, 13 of Britain's top chairmen and chief executives talk about their experiences of this recession and how they see the business environment changing in the future. Each has addressed a wide range of questions designed to provide food for thought for anyone interested in industry and commerce. They also talk openly on more personal subjects: what they like and dislike about their roles, their strengths, their weaknesses, the importance of family life, and so on.

Naturally, some industries were more affected than others by the tough economic conditions, so while some organisations were able to get away with a bit of fine-tuning, others have had to take fairly drastic steps. During the preparation of this book, at a time when many people believed an upturn was just around the corner, Peter Gummer, chairman of Shandwick, took the opposite view and decided that 1992 was going to be even worse than the previous year. He looked at the worst level of fees imaginable and took radical cost-cutting measures, with the result that Shandwick warned it expected to make a pre-tax loss of £1m in the 15 months to the end of October 1991.

The reaction from the Press was predictably hostile. The decision to write off costs associated with business under negotiation, rather than to rely on that business materializing in the coming year, appeared in one paper as 'Several million pounds more has been spent chasing new business that failed to materialize.' Another article made references to Peter Gummer scanning the public relations handbook for tips. In other words, realistic actions taken in order to secure the future of the company, based on a pessimistic forecast of the economic climate ahead, were conveyed to readers, who naturally include shareholders, as signs of failure.

Shandwick's share price dropped rapidly from 125p to 52½p after its announcement. Whether confidence was shaken further by the way in which events were reported is anybody's guess, but the shares subsequently fell to just below 30p. There is no doubt that companies can be made or broken by media coverage, be it fair or otherwise. And it is a peculiarly British tendency to want people to fail. America has its cheerleaders; we, for some reason, have booleaders instead. Small wonder, then, that the participants in this book tend not to gravitate towards the limelight, preferring to keep their heads down and get on with running their businesses. The biographical information at the top of each chapter was prepared from the information available on their CVs: Robert Louis-Dreyfus's consisted of 31 words. But then, Robert Louis-Dreyfus has a love-hate relationship with the Press. 'I bet if you did a poll of businessmen who have been featured in front page articles, most of them are failures within five years,' he says.

Having to make redundancies is painful for all concerned, but, as Jon Foulds (of the Halifax) points out, it is better to do it all in one go. If the exercise happens repeatedly the organization feels as if it is dying the death of a thousand cuts. Shandwick got all its bad news over in one fell swoop, and in his chapter, Peter Gummer talks candidly about the events leading up to his announcement. It is interesting to learn that he found other chapters of *A Head For Business* changed the way he viewed the actions he was taking. If the chairman of the largest public relations group in the world can find the advice given in this book useful, it should certainly be of value to those of us who are rather less experienced.

Some of the companies that got into difficulty during this recession had over-diversified. When Robert Louis-Dreyfus joined Saatchi & Saatchi in 1990, his first task was to focus back on the company's core business and dispose of peripheral acquisitions at a time when the downturn was already upon us. He talks of the dangers of diversification and gives advice on how to expand sensibly. Though TI Group had also diversified, Christopher Lewinton was brought into the company in 1986, in time to embark on a strategy designed to cope with circumstances such as a recession before they actually arrived. By concentrating on the company's core business he was able to turn TI Group into a world-leader in engineering.

It seems that 'understand your industry' is going to be one of the key phrases of the 1990s. More importance will be attached to strategy than ever before, with companies increasingly focusing on what they know best. Not that Sir Owen Green believes too much in focus: 'I call it hocus pocus', he says. 'We don't have mission statements at BTR, though we do have core business – that which is left after the apple is eaten!' Sir Owen's down-to-earth style of leadership has turned what was a small rubber company into a highly profitable international group, though even BTR has suffered its first setback after 23 years of successive profit. 'We thought we were recession-resistant to a greater extent than has proved to be the case,' he says.

If any industry can be truly recession-resistant, it has to be pharmaceuticals. As Robert Bauman points out, people are still going to fall ill, medicines are still going to be prescribed and, in many countries of the world, governments are going to keep on paying for them. Consequently, SmithKline Beecham has been less affected than most other organizations. Not that there is any room for complacency; Robert Bauman believes they can increase production by fostering a culture where everyone strives for continuous improvement. 'By doing that, no matter what happens, we're going to be in a better position than our competitors,' he says.

For Elwyn Eilledge of Ernst & Young, it was the first time in his career that professional services were hit by a recession. The thought of accountancy firms having a redundancy programme was entirely new. Meanwhile, the Halifax Building Society figures for 1991 showed the highest level of mortgage arrears in its history, and Lloyds Bank was hit harder than ever before. Of course, on top of the recession we had the Gulf War, which had dramatic and far-reaching effects on many industries as flights, holidays and conferences were cancelled. 'A lot of our customers are in the leisure business, and in some cases their sales dropped by 90 per cent,' says Brian Pitman, explaining the effect the war had on Lloyds. Sir Colin Marshall and Geoffrey Maitland Smith talk in their chapters about its impact on British Airways and Sears.

For both Courtaulds and Courtaulds Textiles, the recession of the early 1980s was far worse than the present one. The drastic actions that Sir Christopher Hogg was forced to take meant that Courtaulds emerged fitter, leaner and more efficient, so that by the time this one came around, the business was in an altogether better shape. The reality is that it often takes a crisis such as a recession to force people to take actions they had been putting off during the heady days of the boom. 'You can reduce your costs and reshape your organization better than at any other time,' says Sir Robert Scholey. 'Your people understand the changes you are making. They don't like them, but they know they are necessary.'

Sir Robert believes the manufacturing base in Britain is certainly too weak; a sentiment shared by Christopher Lewinton. 'We're the only G7 nation that denigrates its engineers and treats them as second-class citizens, hence we don't attract the best brains. If you don't get the best brains into industry, you don't create the wealth,' he says, and in future wants to see the industrial world, the academic world and government working much more closely with each other.

Education is the key to industrial success in the future, according to Sir Graham Day. 'British companies don't fail as a result of foreign competitors invading. Opportunities are created because people haven't caught up with what is happening in the global market,' he says. Too often, the losers are those with an inadequate educational base for the majority of their employees. To counteract this problem, Rover alone now spends 7.5 per cent of pay roll – £35m a year – on education and training.

It is rather extraordinary to note that if Europe already had a single currency, Cadbury Schweppes would have saved £6m in transaction fees in 1991 alone. Under the circumstances, it is hardly surprising that Sir Graham has little patience with those who try to link currency with sovereignty.

In *A Head For Business*, each chairman and chief executive gives his views on the impact of the globalization of markets.

The manager of the 1990s has got to be more international than ever before. 'The real success is to have a British or American manager who – before he is 40 – has worked in two or three different cultures for several years,' says Christopher Lewinton. 'He will have come back with an understanding of those different cultures, so when he hires somebody to run the various businesses, he knows what he's doing.'

Lewinton points out that the difference between this recession and previous ones is that in the past there has always been an engine in the world to drive us out. This time there isn't, because the three main players – America, Germany and Japan – are consumed with their own problems. The companies that will best survive are those that can cope with a period of very slow growth for some years to come.

Of course, recessions do come to an end, and rather than just struggling to survive, we should be getting ourselves into shape so we're ready to take advantage of new opportunities as and when they appear. 'My view is that we're close to the bottom already, but there's a lag in time during which people believe these rotten conditions are going to go on for ever. They get terribly gloomy and you have to try and lift them out of it,' says Brian Pitman.

There's no doubt that a sense of humour is vital in order to stay the course. 'When life is this difficult you have to have a sense of humour just to keep matters in perspective,' says Peter Gummer. 'You must remain confident and optimistic, and even if you're not actually having a good time, you can gain real satisfaction from knowing that you are doing the best for the long-term health of your company.'

# 1

# Robert Bauman

## Chief Executive, SmithKline Beecham

*Robert Bauman is Chief Executive of SmithKline Beecham, the company formed in July 1989 when Beecham Group merged with SmithKline Beckman. Born in 1931, he received a bachelor's degree from Ohio Wesleyan University in 1953 and a master's degree from Harvard Business School two years later. He spent 23 years with General Foods, where he became Executive Vice-President and Director in 1972, and President of International operations in 1974. From 1981 to 1985 he was Chairman and Chief Executive of Avco Corporation, a conglomerate in financial services and aerospace. He then served as Vice-Chairman of Textron Inc before joining Beecham Group in 1986 as Executive Chairman. He is also a Director of Capital Cities Communications/ABC, Union Pacific Corporation and CIGNA Corporation.*

The 1980s was the era of huge expansion and great takeovers, but that's all over for now. For those who were expanding it was a very exciting time, and a lot of events were made even more exciting by the Press. But will history look back at the 1980s and say 'That was the decade of great building of competitive capacity and advantage for the United States and Britain?' I don't think so. Certainly not by comparison to attitudes in Germany or Japan.

There's no doubt that this rapid growth had to be corrected, because it couldn't have been sustained, but we should be concerned that it took a recession to slow the economy down. It would have been nice if we could have controlled it through discipline; unfortunately, it never happens like that. Most companies like to think they are capable of constantly improving themselves, but the statistics suggest that it takes facing a crisis to make them do so. It's a principle of nature that only the strong survive. The question is, how can we find some way of monitoring the economy so we don't allow things to go so far that a crisis becomes inevitable?

SmithKline Beecham was affected less by the recession than most organizations, because health care doesn't suffer the same impact.

People are still going to prescribe medicines, and, in many countries around the world, the governments are going to keep paying for them.

We are also in consumer products, primarily over-the-counter medicines. Again, if people have colds and infections, they're going to want to take something to make them feel better, and they will place that need ahead of other items on their list of purchase priority. It's one of the last things in their spectrum of buying power that they're going to eliminate, so for that reason, we are less impacted.

What has affected us is that governments are very concerned about the mounting increase in their costs for health-care services. In every country around the world they are looking to see how they can reduce that growth. They're looking at hospitals, physicians, the pharmaceutical drugs sector and so on, and that has more of an impact on us, particularly in some countries, than an economic recession. It affects the entire industry, and we have to take that into account in our planning.

We anticipated that there would be a recession, but we assumed that our products would come through it. We felt there could be some impact on selected businesses, but that it would be minor, so it didn't cause us to make any fundamental changes to our strategies, and our profits have continued quite well. Any actions we have taken have been part of a long-term programme to increase productivity, so we are fostering a culture in which everyone strives for continuous improvement. We believe by doing that, no matter what happens, we're going to be in a better position than our competitors. We'll be in a position to grow, and we'll be ready to accept and manage change.

History has shown that everything runs in cycles, and I think that will always be the case, so you have to live as if there were going to be cycles in everything you do. The question is, how do you prepare yourself for them? A lot of people do not like change; it worries them, it makes them unsure. But change is about doing things better, and that's much more exciting to me than just doing the same old thing. If you can deal with change, you can deal with cycles; even the cycles you may not predict.

We all want to be smart enough to be able to predict the future. I would like us to have much better forecasting systems so we would be able to anticipate the cycles more effectively, but that's not likely. For example, at the end of the Gulf War, when oil prices shot up, it established a whole different set of economics. Who could have predicted that? Possibly we could have had a better insight into some of these events, but we can't assume we're going to predict every one. We've all got to be prepared for something unexpected to happen.

In business everyone is affected at some time or other by these cycles, or other problems. Some people say 'Well, they don't happen that frequently, and they happen to others, not to me, so I'll just manage as usual.' I think that's a mistake. If you're going to do something dynamic and push your company forward, you've got to strive to do better than just survive. You've got to create a positive atmosphere in which you can become by far the most productive company in your industry sector.

You must assume in your planning that there are going to be difficulties, and you must ask yourself what you can learn from them. What can you do to reduce the impact? How can you best manage through these difficulties? You should make sure you are operating in such a superior fashion that you can manage better than any-body else, and be successful through whatever contingencies you encounter. Your management must be ready to deal with change and the dynamics of the market place. If you can accomplish all of that you will be in the best position to continue to succeed.

Some problems are self-created. For example, every organization tends to have herding instincts; it's only natural to watch and follow what other people do, and in the late 1960s and during the 1970s, everybody had to diversify. Towards the end of the 1970s companies diversified too far, so they started to focus on their core business again. Then we moved into the 1980s, and people were looking for growth. Times were good and consumers had confidence. The banks were looking for growth, too; there was easy money available – lots of money – the banks were prepared to give it to you, almost. They were giving companies more than their assets were worth, or without any security at all. Everyone got caught up with heavy spending and carried on as if things were never going to change. Then, when we hit bad times, companies which had gone too far and hadn't kept their eyes on the cash got into difficulty, particularly those which had taken on debt.

There's absolutely nothing wrong with taking on debt as long as you have sufficient cash to cover the interest. So the biggest lesson to learn is that you have to make sure you manage your cash, because companies that manage their cash will come through a recession better. One can't blame the banks; it was just a combination of herding instincts, free and easy money, the fact that times were good for growth, and that everyone wanted to participate in that growth. Consequently, they over-extended themselves.

Certainly this recession is going to be a great lesson for people starting up new businesses. The banks will remind them – everybody's going to remind them – and they're probably going to be more aware of the impact of going too far too fast. But memories dim, and it won't be long before they are following the herding instincts again.

For the entrepreneurs the latter half of the 1980s was a very glamorous period. Looking at the success they had in developing their products and finding a niche, they obviously had some good strategies. So what went wrong from a strategic point of view? Perhaps they didn't have a sound enough financial strategy. For a while what they were doing during this period of growth was not at all bad. They just tried to do too much without having the financial understanding. You can't necessarily blame them; many of these entrepreneurs were quite young and had never been through a recession, so they weren't thinking about the bad times. When you're growing so fast and things are going well, it's not easy to sit down and think 'Wait a minute, I'd better slow down.' In fact, it's very difficult. Obviously, in hindsight, they should have paid more attention to the cash flow they were generating in relation to the speed of expansion, and not gone beyond that. But I don't think they were stupid; in fact, they were extremely bright and still are.

We should never discourage the entrepreneurial spirit which is so critical for the creation of jobs and for the health of the economy. We've got to foster that spirit, but at the same time, banks who are dealing with young companies should monitor their cash flow and their security, and if indeed they are growing too fast. I don't expect many of us were given a blank cheque at the age of 12, nor should a young company be. In future there to be more attention paid to the value and importance of cash.

The recession should have reminded people that cash, though not the single most important thing, is just as important as profits. There is a tendency, in my opinion, for companies to get preoccupied with profits. They believe that the way they get value for shareholders as a public company is to improve profits, because that is what the market-place talks about. But the majority of analysts will agree that the best correlation to share prices is free cash flow. The problem is, it isn't easy to determine free cash flow, because of accounting systems and the different ways in which companies report. So they take a short cut, showing earnings per share, because that is the biggest factor affecting free cash flow. Then they get into bad habits, because when interest rates shoot up, they need that cash.

For example, if people running a sales organization are chasing profits, they want to carry a lot of stock, because they never want to have to worry about running out. Well, that's fine for profits, but not for cash, because that's a lot of inventory they're building up. The people in the purchasing department are going to buy at the lowest possible price per unit, because that gives them the highest possible profit margin. If they can buy 1,000 at ten cents, or 5,000 at nine cents, they're going to buy 5,000 because it helps their profits, but that ties up their cash. All these things can work against one another, so the drive should always be on cash. Companies got carried away and forgot about the importance of cash, but now they're paying much more attention to it.

Some talk about cutting capital or spending as a defence against recession, but if you are too conservative in order to protect yourself, you're going to lose your competitive position. You can cut back and delay on your capital spending, get tough on your inventory and so on, but if you're running a very tight inventory already, you will have less of a need to do that. And you should be running a very tight inventory every day. Why wait until a recession?

For the rest of the 1990s I think we're all going to go back to the fundamentals. Cash, sound management practices, doing a better job than your competitors . . . that type of approach. It's very necessary, because there are real opportunities for substantial improvement in productivity to achieve competitive advantage in other countries. We should be paying a lot more attention to what is going on in Japan. Japan's excellent companies are able to come over to the United States or the UK, put a plant up and achieve the same productivity and efficiencies as they can in Japan. All they need is two or three Japanese managers who understand their management systems; the rest of the employees are American or British. Yet comparable plants run by Americans or by the British can't achieve the same results. It's not because the Japanese are Japanese, it is because they are using very sound management practices. So I think we're going to see a lot more concentration on how to manage, how to drive for competitive advantage and increased productivity.

The majority of organizations are going to have to make a lot of adjustments in order to cope with the globalization of markets. Industries like ours will be less affected because we compete globally already; it's the only way we can operate. Others are going to have to start discovering new ways, and in the long-term it will make them more efficient. But the increased competition is likely to be to result in more and more mergers. For hi-tech organizations – and I define them as ones which spend more than 10 per cent of sales on research and development – there is a heavy investment programme. It takes ten years usually from the day you start research for the product to reach the market-place. To develop that product costs anything from £50m to £100m, and it's a high risk because you don't know whether it is going to be successful. At the time of our merger in 1989, we were the first company in our industry to consolidate. Since then, four others have also merged, and that trend is going to continue because research and development activity is so huge that organizations cannot carry it all on their own.

Everyone in industry ought to be asking themselves 'What do we need to do more of in the 1990s to be more successful than we were in the 1980s?' Business schools, by definition, should be creating new thoughts and concepts which will result in new business opportunities, and create competitive advantage for the next generation. But most of them tend to use case studies, picking up on the practice of the day, which is not necessarily going to provide students with insights into the future. These can be provided if students are taught by brilliant people who are capable of opening their minds to new concepts, and I suspect there are some very brilliant teachers around, but business schools aren't automatically the answer to best management practices for the future.

The style of management in the 1980s was all about delegation. It meant that if you were given a profit goal, you delegated it to someone else, checked on him once in a while to see how he was getting on, and, therefore, you were a good manager. But good management is about being involved; getting people to participate together and to understand how they're moving forward, what they're trying to achieve, the risks they're taking . . . the risks they're not taking. All that gets lost if you over-delegate. It's adding layers of management without increasing effectiveness. In fact, you're almost walking away from your responsibilities.

People who work for you will still want you to delegate. They'll say 'Don't you have trust in me? I'm a good guy, tell me what you want me to do and I'll do it,' but that's not the point. The point is, can someone help somebody else? Perhaps the one who has been there longer is not the one who is actually in charge; it may be someone younger who is employed at a higher level. Let's say he really needs some help; maybe with a little more dialogue, there could be some better decisions. This concept of 'You don't trust me if you don't delegate' is a bad one, and throughout the 1990s I think we'll see an emphasis on having fewer management levels, so that there are fewer managers, but those there are will be more involved and have greater responsibility.

It's very easy to say that a successful manager is one who is willing to demonstrate and deliver leadership, but what is leadership? I think a leader is a person who has the ability to have some sense of what is happening, has a vision of the future, and is able to capture that vision and bring it alive to the organization. A leader is one who clearly sees the objectives and strategies, and can help others to see them too. I have never heard of a successful Olympic swimmer who just goes out to swim. He has to set targets for himself, and every time he achieves them, he's got to set new ones. Each new objective should require just the right amount of stretch, but it shouldn't be so hard that he gives up and decides to try another sport. A manager's got to find that balance, and he's got to have the strategy that's going to take him to where he wants to go. Then he's got to make sure his objectives and strategies are accepted and adopted by the company. Don't just delegate: you have to be a participant in the process. What are the plans? Have you tried that? The last aspect of leadership deals with the people in your organization. You must have people who are the best and provide them with the opportunity to train and get into the spirit of the company. The leader is the one who can transform the whole organization, and ultimately his strategy will become part of the culture.

But you have to make sure you have the right strategies: in other words, you don't want so many new strategies that the organization can't pursue them. Strategies have to be specific enough to drive direction, and they have to have ownership. If people feel they are part of those strategies, they will be far more effective. Share option plans help give a feeling of participating in the rewards, but an organization will be more successful if its people are part of developing the strategy. It's human nature to feel much more motivated if we're part of developing something. If we're part of developing it, we will then want to execute it; if someone says 'Here is your strategy, go do it,' it's not the same. Ownership and involvement in those strategies are of fundamental importance, and that is not going to change.

Some managers have a tendency not to listen to the people who work with them. Instead of participating, too many times it's the other way round and they say 'Here's what I think you ought to do.' There isn't enough honest, two-way communication, therefore there isn't enough trust. You also miss out on ideas; people closest to the work are often the ones who know how to improve it best. You need to participate, you need to work together. Targets should be shared: what are we trying to do? How can we best achieve it? That sort of attitude helps mutual agreement and ownership of objectives and strategies. I'm a great believer in dialogue. What do you talk about with the people who report to you? Is it what the results are? Or is it how the results are achieved? I believe very strongly in talking about the latter. It's not only what you did, but also how you did it, because that's where the lessons are learned, that's where the ongoing capability is developed, and ultimately that's how one sustains good results . . . by having a standard process.

If you can do all these things, you'll be successful at managing through a crisis. If you have a team of people working effectively together and cross-functioning, they will constantly be asking themselves how they can perform better. Maybe next week they'll find a new way to improve. Compare them with a team of people who say 'This is our process. Until someone tells us differently, we'll continue as we are.' In the event of a crisis, the first team will look at how to do things better. They may have to step up the urgency a touch, but they won't panic.

As a leader, I've been reasonably good at picking people. I have demanded the very best, and have succeeded in motivating them; this is one of my strengths. But if my peers and subordinates have criticism of me, it's that I don't celebrate our successes enough. I will refer to them, but I'll usually qualify it with about six other things we could do better in the future. I think that is fair criticism; sometimes I get too preoccupied with trying to do things better.

Personally, I'm a great believer in taking a lot of exercise; to me it's a great way of relaxing, and of focusing the mind. I love playing tennis and golf, though I don't have as much time for them as I would like, but on vacation I do play every day. My family is very important to me; we're very close and we do a lot together. I also have a love of plants; before I came to the UK I had cultivated and raised more than a thousand orchids of various varieties, mostly cymbidiums and phalaenopsis.

If I look back, I think I've been reasonably successful. There are very few things I would do differently if I had my time over again, because I have really enjoyed the opportunity to be associated with so many industries. Some years ago I read a book called *Self Renewal* by John Gardner (Norton, 1983), and one of the basic principles was that any organization must change itself every ten years. As an individual, one needs to put oneself into new situations in order to have stimulation and new sets of challenges. It's equally important for an organization to have people who are capable of producing those challenges. I've been lucky in that every ten years I have been exposed to a totally new and different challenge, and for me it has been very stimulating.

## TIPS FOR SUCCESS

- Assume, in your planning, that there will be stumbling blocks along the way. Be sure that you are operating in a way that is superior, enabling you to handle these problems better than anyone else.

- Be ready to deal with change, then you'll be ready to deal with unexpected events.

- Remember that free cash flow is as important as profits.

- Employ only the very best people and provide them with the opportunity to train.

- Make sure your objectives and strategies are accepted and adopted within the company. Don't just delegate; be a participant in the process. Targets should be shared.

- As a leader, act as you say; continue to learn, to grow, to change, and encourage and support others to do the same.

# 2
# Sir Graham Day

*Chairman, Cadbury Schweppes, PowerGen, Crombie*
*Insurance (UK), Interim Chairman, British Aerospace*

*Sir Graham Day is Chairman of Cadbury Schweppes, PowerGen*
*and Crombie Insurance (UK). In 1991 he became Interim*
*Chairman of British Aerospace, prior to which he was a Non-*
*Executive Director and the Chairman of Rover. He is Deputy*
*Chairman of MAI and a Director of British Aerospace, the Laird*
*Group, Thorn EMI and Altnacraig Shipping. In addition he is*
*on the board of various overseas companies in countries such as*
*Canada, Luxembourg and The Netherlands. Sir Graham was*
*educated at Dalhousie University in Halifax, Canada, and*
*practised Law before joining Canadian Pacific in 1964.*

For those of us who were managers in the 1970s, the 1990s are
looking quite familiar. The various techniques we learned, or thought
we had learned, we are having to deploy again. Those who learnt
them in the 1970s and chose to forget them in the 1980s are having
to learn them all over again, and it is very expensive. But for those,
God bless them, who are younger than we are, and who are learning
for the first time in the 1990s, it is just as painful as it was for us in
the 1970s.

They have found the recession quite emotionally destabilizing, and
have had no way of knowing what to do. But it's like Shadrach,
Meshach and Abednigo . . . you've got to push managers through the
fiery furnace at some stage in their careers. If you don't have a
genuine external threat like a recession, when you can actually blood
your younger managers, you almost have to devise circumstances to
test their performance. You have to know how resilient they are
before you trust them with more responsibility.

The management of PowerGen – the smaller of the two privatized
CEGB conventional generating children – has learned a lot from this
recession. Many of them are very young and consequently weren't
managing in the 1970s, but each non-executive member of the board
is very experienced and has been through it all before, so we were

able to pass on our observations. The company has an increasingly strong balance sheet as a result of the way in which the business has developed managerially and the costs have been controlled.

Cadbury Schweppes is a global business, therefore it is less likely to be hit hard by a recession in a couple of markets. The company has outstandingly good management both in terms of overall competence and individual ability, and the cost base has always been gripped very tightly under Dominic Cadbury. This combination of geographical diversity and quality of management has seen profits grow during a period when sales have been generally flat, so Cadbury Schweppes has not been as negatively affected as many others.

British Aerospace has a very diverse portfolio. The military aircraft business had a pretty good year in 1991, whereas the property and automobile businesses have suffered. Other businesses, those involved with weapons and communications for instance, have had a difficult time not because of the recession, but because of the 'peace dividend'. Structurally, the world has changed.

You can never anticipate a recession precisely, but you have to try and see it coming. In Rover we took a fairly pessimistic view in June 1990 of not merely the UK market but others as well, and decided the objective was to manage for cash so we could continue to re-invest in the business. The recession has been deeper and longer than we thought it would be at the time, but our strategy has seen Rover through it. Not without some pain, and not without a lot of concern about when the market is going to recover, but generally we got it right. Rover's UK market share and the number of exports have actually increased, despite the fact that its volume is down. In profitability, Rover performed better in the second half of 1991 than in the first half, and whilst overall there was a loss, its cash position has remained broadly neutral.

When costs become out of line in relation to your sales and profit margins, hacking them back can be very painful. Memories, of course, fade, so if you take your hand off the control valve when the economy is expanding and let the costs get fat again, sooner or later you will have to repeat the exercise, and then it will have been painful twice. Good management, such as that of Cadbury Schweppes, has kept a grip on its costs. They never got out of line, so whilst the knob may have been tightened a couple of notches, it wasn't as bad as it might have been. In each organization we have had to make manpower reductions, but in the broadest sense of the word. Depending on the strength of your pension fund you can give people the option of retiring earlier, so one tries to use financial mechanisms to encourage people to leave on a voluntary basis. It is better for the individuals than being made redundant, and certainly better for the economy.

During a period of expansion it is easy to build up activities around the perimeter which don't appear to do you a lot of harm, but the fact is, they might not do you a lot of good either. All of a sudden, when the recession comes, you say 'I can't afford to do this. At best, it may be a good long-term proposition, but it is absorbing a lot of my cash.' Cash is always king, so you end up backing out, but it needn't happen if you control your focus in the first place. You have to sit down and say 'What is my business all about?' You have to review your strategy constantly and remind yourself where your corporate roots are.

In British Aerospace we published a prospectus in connection with the rights issue which indicated where we're concentrating and where we're not, so we're going to be addressing some of the non-core businesses. I suppose in British Aerospace historical corporate terms that might be deemed to be radical, but I don't think it is. It means we're controlling our focus. In a well-managed business, unless your back is right to the wall, you shouldn't have to take radical steps during a recession.

Managers, like all other human beings, don't have any immortality. But perhaps the ultimate immortality which a manager may be deemed to have is the quality of the subordinates he leaves behind. When I was with Canadian Pacific I worked for a man named Les Smith; the son of a Scottish immigrant. Even today, there are maybe seven of us who call ourselves 'Les Smith's boys'. He wasn't an easy man to work for but he was an extremely good manager. And whatever I do, if I look back, invariably I realize that I have done it because of Les Smith. In other words, I would say Les Smith was a successful manager, because under his guidance he spawned at least seven of us. He was the senior operating vice-president of Canadian Pacific Railway, and he is fondly remembered by all of us because of what we learned from him. We've all done fairly well, and I hope he takes some satisfaction from that.

The old Canadian Pacific rule is that there are only two important matters in business; one is people, the other is money, but in that order. So the successful manager, above all else, is someone who identifies, encourages and promotes good people. Your ability to pick good people is very important. Frankly, you try and pick people who are better than you. If your ego can't stand that, you probably aren't going to survive as a manager.

One of the differences between the 1980s and the 1990s is that organizations are becoming much flatter, because thick organizations are expensive. So we're giving much more authority, right down to the lowest level of each organization. We're actually trusting people to do more. As long as it isn't illegal, immoral or fattening, they can reach their objectives in the way they see fit, providing they achieve the financial result.

Cash is the only four-letter word which forgives all business sins . . . if you have enough of it. In the 1980s one was able to run the cycle faster and faster. For too many, the attitude was 'Hell, I can finance it. Forget the balance sheet; look at the profit and loss . . . this is a growth company.' It was bicycle management; everything was all right as long as you were peddling. All of a sudden people forgot the discipline of controlling the cash, because they were always financing the next move. But you couldn't in the 1970s, and you sure as hell can't in the 1990s. That, I think, is one of the essential differences which people are having to relearn. It's not what you can finance, it's what you can repay. Balance sheets are back in style.

In the 1980s, the banks were running around saying 'Pssst . . . can I loan you a few million?' Niche market operators like Sock Shop expanded, riding on the crest of an idea, and they forgot about the cash. When companies fold they blame the banks for turning off their lines of credit, they blame the recession or say they over-expanded, but fundamentally it gets back to planning. It means they didn't have a grip on their business.

Unbelievably, there are still some companies who do not do strategic planning. If they do, it's a delegated exercise and everybody ignores it. Maybe it says more about me than anything else, but I am distinctly uncomfortable if I am in circumstances where there isn't a plan. So how do you begin to formulate strategies? In order to do a corporate planning exercise, you have to work with two pools of data. One is the 'environmental scan': an external view of your industry worldwide, analysis of the competition, estimates of the economic developments of countries where you may be operating, and their stability. If you are doing business in the Middle East, how stable is it? If you are reliant on that geographical business, do you have contingency plans?

The other pool of data which you have to deal with is the 'operational audit', an internal assessment; an attempt to look at your business, warts and all. It's like having a semi-public confessional, and if you deceive yourself it can be fatal. It is the chief executive's job to make sure that planning is done. He can delegate many of the component tasks, but he can't ever back away from the responsibility for the planning process, driving through decisions on key strategies and subsequently ensuring that they are implemented.

The difference, as we approach the 21st century, is the scale of the environmental scan, the externalities. I hate to use that trite word 'global', but it doesn't matter how big or small your company is, or whether you're competing directly with the global giants, the fact is, their behaviour impacts on the way in which you do business. Demands which customers place on manufacturers and suppliers of goods and services are steadily increasing, but the meeting of those demands by the global players creates an environment in which a small regional player also has to compete. General standards are being raised, and the speed of the planning process is of vital importance. You think, you plan, you execute . . . but you have to do it quickly. Things are changing so rapidly that you can't drag your feet.

The companies which, having got through the thinking and the planning, take a lead and act quickly will be the winners. In Rover we talk about being a fast follower. In a couple of instances, like our low-pressure sand casting of aluminium components for the K-series engine, we're a leader. Quite frankly we had no choice, but it was a high-risk technical and engineering commitment. Fundamentally we prefer to be a fast follower, which, in management terms, has us embracing the philosophy of speed. In other words, we respond very, very quickly. If you're a leader you have to be able to accept the financial and operational risk of getting it wrong, and I don't think Rover can. A huge company can afford to get it wrong a number of times, because when they get it right, the scale of operation will outweigh all the other losses.

Meanwhile, higher standards arising out of internationalization are hitting people in business without them even knowing. If you're in the assembly business, as Rover is, and you're trying to get the message through to a relatively small supplier about its performance and standards, you may be utterly incomprehensible to that firm because its experience is so confined. British companies don't fail as a result of foreign competitors invading. People don't just parachute into Britain and establish plants here. The opportunities are created because the local guys haven't caught up with what's happening in the global market. They haven't bothered to notice what is happening to standards.

When internationalization bites you may not even see the teeth closing, but the companies which are internationalizing most successfully are those which come from a secure base in their domestic situation. They are able to take their people and their culture, cherry-pick the best in some of the other countries and compete very effectively. Too many times the loser is the domestic business which has an inadequate educational base for the vast majority of its employees. 'School-leaver' in Britain today means '16 and uneducated'. People ask 'What are the opportunities for school-leavers?' I say the answer is zero. They're going to be on the scrap heap of the unemployed, and it's going to get worse before it gets better.

Rover now spends 7.5 per cent of pay roll – some £35m a year – on education and training. If this was Germany, we'd only have to spend £5m. We'd have that £30m drop into our profit. We don't spend it because we're nice people and it's altruistic, we do it because we have no choice. Our people are as intelligent and adaptable as any workforce in the world, but person for person, against the competition, they're not as well educated. We, with their co-operation, are trying to do something about that. Politicians keep talking about the importance of training, but you can't train people until they're educated. And I'm not talking about manual skills, I'm talking about grafting operational skills on to a solid, educational base.

Recently we had a visit from the All-Party Motor Vehicle Committee of the House of Commons and House of Lords. We showed them the new K-series engine line and said they could talk to any of our employees. They saw one man, standing at a work-station, clearly doing absolutely nothing. It was fascinating; I knew just what was in their minds. Eventually one of them went up to him and asked what he was doing. So the chap, who was in his early 50s, said 'On a good day, if everything works perfectly, I should have to do nothing. It used to be,' and he held up his hands, 'that I was paid for using these.' Then he touched his temple and said 'I'm now paid for using this. My job is to anticipate when something is likely to go wrong,' and he went on to explain what that might be, how he would identify it, and what he would do in consequence. If I'd written the man a script he couldn't have delivered it better, because he articulated the shift in the business from someone who was a skilled tradesman to someone who, after being retrained, was using his powers of observation, processing that information and taking remedial action when necessary.

Education is one of the things which either enables companies to internationalize, or impedes their internationalization. I found it extremely reassuring when visiting Japanese car plants to see that they put people first and technology second. They've been very careful where they put their capital, and they're convinced that in many instances human intervention does a better job.

Companies doing business in Europe have to be ahead of what is happening on the ground so the benefits can roll through. You don't want the benefits to be there as a potential, then have to adjust your business to secure them. You want to be there in anticipation. I am very keen to have a common currency. If there had been a common currency in 1991, Cadbury Schweppes would have saved at least £6m in transaction costs. Every business trading in Europe would save a lot of money, so I have absolutely zero patience with those who try to link sovereignty with currency. Currency is a commodity; it facilitates trade, nothing more.

Ultimately the consumer is going to get more choice, good prices, and better service as a result of the Single Market, but there are great conflicts between what politicians are saying and what their countries are actually doing. They start with the political objectives and fail to recognize that they have to be translated into reality. So there is a tremendous amount of political bullshit, while many people who commercially are totally in favour of 1992 are struggling to make it happen. The principal downside I fear in practical terms is the growth of European bureaucracy. Life is going to become infinitely more complex, and if you are involved in strategic planning, your assessment of external factors is going to have to incorporate more of what is happening in Europe, when it is likely to happen, and how it is going to affect you. I think that's very difficult.

If I have a fetish in business, it is planning, and I think that is one of my strengths. It's not that I don't take risks, just that I seldom make a move before I've thought it through. People think I'm hasty, that I shoot from the hip, but we debate these moves *ad nauseam* before taking action. I don't always signal, and it may look like instant execution, but it never is. Another strength is that I'm honest, therefore when we have been financially in a tight corner, I, and the organization for which I am speaking, have been given the benefit of the doubt, because those on the other side of the table know that I would not knowingly mislead them.

I'm a good people picker, and I take a lot of satisfaction in seeing the people I have identified and promoted prosper. I've been fortunate in working with people who are younger and brighter than I am, and I find that very stimulating. I've always been prepared to gamble on people who are quite young, and I don't take too much notice of CVs. If someone says they've got 20 years' experience, it may be one year's experience 20 times. I'm more concerned with what kind of jobs they have had.

One of my fundamental weaknesses for some of the positions I've held is my generalist background; my education is humanities and law, and that's a little risky because I've been managing heavy engineering companies for a lot of my life. Had I been an engineer, maybe I could have done some things better and faster, and been less reliant in a difficult situation on someone whose judgement I didn't know if I could trust. But I can put my hand on my heart and honestly say that I have never stopped studying since I joined Canadian Pacific. I'd been out of law school for eight years when all of a sudden I was having to examine witnesses who were expert on fiscal matters. I realized I couldn't cope with the economics so I started to grind through basic texts, and since that little lesson, which I learnt almost too late, I have continued to study in order keep up to date. I do it in a very systematic way, early in the morning and late at night, and I think that is very important.

Personal image is both a blessing and a curse. Sometimes I'll delay taking a hard personnel decision. Sometimes I've actually increased the business risk because I wanted to be morally satisfied that the relationship wasn't going to work, and that's a weakness. In other words, I'm too soft. But people see me as a hard son of a bitch; that's what the media say anyway. It's a curse in that you keep wanting to jump up and down and say 'No, I'm not like that,' but image is a function of leadership.

Some managers are utterly faceless. In a large, stable organization they can function extremely effectively, but in a crisis people have to follow you on faith even if they hate what you're trying to do, and maybe your image helps. Early in the Rover days, when it was British Leyland, I heard a chap say as we were walking out of a meeting 'I knew we were in difficulty but I didn't think things were bad enough to have to bring in that son of a bitch.' He obviously didn't realize I was just ahead of him, but I thought to myself 'That's OK, because what he has inferred is that things are really bad.' Sometimes, not only *is* there a crisis, but also you have to jump up and down and say 'Hey, there is a crisis.'

The most common mistake having identified a crisis is not deciding what to do. The first thing you must do is identify the way forward; my bear story illustrates the point. Three chaps were in a ramshackle shed in the Canadian woods when a vast grizzly bear attacked. There was no way that the shed was going to be able to withstand it. This was a crisis. Two of the chaps were milling around trying to determine what they should do. The third guy got his running shoes on and prepared to go out the back window, so the other two said 'What are you doing? You'll never outrun the bear.' And he said 'I don't intend to outrun the bear. I only have to outrun one of you.' In other words, he knew there was a crisis, identified a key issue and solution, and was implementing it.

If you're at the apex of a corporate pyramid and there's a crisis, you have to identify the critical issues. In my experience there are never more than three and usually only two. Then you say to your subordinates 'The only two things I'm interested in are A and B. Whatever else happens, you deal with it, but if anything comes up on A and B, tell me. We've got to get A and B right, or we're dead.' You need to be approachable because nobody wants to bring you bad news, but they must.

Family life is very important if you want to be successful. I've been married for 34 years, and there's not the slightest doubt in my tiny mind that without this particular woman I wouldn't have survived anywhere near as happily. It's not merely the emotional support; it's the debate. There is nothing I do that I don't debate with Ann. Nothing. Sometimes it's just a monologue because I tend to do a lot of thinking through verbalization, but she has known me so well for so long that she picks up nuances which I perhaps haven't even intended.

In my days as chief executive of Cammell Laird Shipbuilders we had a very good production director who was not an insignificant consumer of Scotland's favourite product. I used to go home and say to Ann 'I don't know what I'm going to do with him. He does a good job, but when his alcohol quotient rises he takes it out on the staff. He's becoming less and less productive.' I agonized over that, and it was Ann who pointed out that his behaviour was colouring everything everybody did, including me. So I told the chairman, Sir David Barratt, that I was going to have to let this chap go, and the dear old man said to me 'Graham, what took you so long?' I asked why he hadn't said anything before, and he said 'If I had, what would you have learned?' The great wisdom of this man, giving me enough rope to get to the bottom of the problem and act on it. But yes, home life is very important.

I've tried very hard to plan the fundamental structure of the family life to provide financial security. Ann runs all the family finances, and has done since the day we were married. She does it extremely well; she's a good manager. My daughters still joke about the family's five-year plans. We have always had dinner-table discussions, even when the kids were very young, and if I was working late Ann would actually hold the meal, because she recognized that it was the time when the family made decisions. When I was asked to become chairman and chief executive of British Shipbuilders in 1983 we had the typical over-dinner discussion, and it was a family decision to return to the UK from Canada.

I like the strategic dimension in my role more than anything else. I like the intellectual exercise of trying to identify not the problems, but The Problem. I think of myself as a short-lister: I always maintain that in any business there are only two or three things that will make or break you. The key is to identify what they are and develop a plan that will contend with them. What I hate is routine. Most of the time it's the minutia that irritate me. I always need someone to clean up after me in an administration sense. I'm a stickler for detail, though I hate to do it myself, and I'm very impatient, particularly when people don't get things done on schedule.

If I could have my time over again, I would not have agreed in 1975 to accept a government appointment as deputy chairman and chief executive of the organizing committee for British Shipbuilders. It was an absolute fiasco. What Labour had in me was someone with value as a manager. What they wanted was a gofer; an administrator who did what he was told. 1976 really was the worst working year of my life; I was totally frustrated and I had no authority. There are all kinds of other things I could have done. If I had written them down on slips of paper, stuck them on the wall and thrown darts at them, any one of them would have been better than that lousy decision.

Otherwise I think I've been successful by my standards in that I've never dropped a major ball, but also I think it's because I was lucky enough to have worked for a really great manager. I believe in the mentor system, and I had a mentor in Les Smith. By contrast, Ian Sinclair, who eventually became chairman of Canadian Pacific, was probably the worst senior I have ever come across. He was immensely bright – multi-faceted in talent terms – but it was like working for the intelligence service; you were seen individually and only told that sliver of information which would at a minimum enable you to do your part of the job. I dearly loved Canadian Pacific, and would have been happy to stay there until my retiring day but for him.

In retrospect it was probably a good thing that I left. The decision to come and work in the UK was the turning point for me, because I went from being an assistant snowball maker to a snowball thrower. In other words, I moved from a staff job to a line job, and I did it at the age of 38, which by my standards was very late. I knew it was a major decision, moving across the North Atlantic with a young family, but it turned out to be a critical one. That single move has affected my life ever since. Now, in a way, I've regressed; I'm back to being an assistant snowball maker, because I'm essentially non-executive. These days I'm helping other people make the snowballs and then cheering as they throw them, but that's what I enjoy.

## TIPS FOR SUCCESS

- Pick people who you believe either intellectually or in terms of specific skills are better than you.

- Think, plan, then execute . . . but do it quickly.

- Test the performance of your people before deploying them at the next level.

- Never stop studying. Keep up to date in the areas where you are trying to function.

- Stay sober. Loose lips sink ships; so when you're being entertained remember it's because somebody is trying to sell you something.

# 3

# Elwyn Eilledge

## *Co-Chairman, Ernst & Young International*

*Elwyn Eilledge is Senior Partner of Ernst & Young UK and Co-Chairman of Ernst & Young International. Born in 1935, he joined the firm at the age of 31 and spent five years working overseas, first in Liberia, then in Hamburg. On returning to the UK in 1972 he became a partner in the London audit department, and in 1983 was appointed Managing Partner of the London office. Two years later he was appointed Deputy Senior Partner of the UK firm, then Senior Partner of Ernst & Whinney in 1986. He became Senior Partner of Ernst & Young in 1989 on the merger of Ernst & Whinney with Arthur Young.*

It is the first time in my career that professional services have been hit by a major recession. The thought of accountancy firms having a redundancy programme was entirely new. For the last quarter of a century we had seen fairly uninterrupted growth in our profession. Redundancies were something that happened to our clients, but never to us. However, the recognition that service firms don't have some God-given right to continue growing while the rest of the economy suffers isn't necessarily a bad thing.

We made about 150 redundancies, which out of 7,500 people may not seem like very many, but it's a lot for the 150 who lost their jobs. The fact that it happened at all was a tremendous shock for the system. We were the first firm of accountants to do it, and most of our competitors followed suit throughout 1991.

Fortunately, firms such as ours have a good level of repeat business, in audit, tax and, to a lesser extent, consultancy. But during a period of recession there are fewer takeover bids, mergers and acquisitions, so all that extra work we're always doing for our clients isn't there in such abundance. Instead, the big growth area is insolvency services: receiverships, administration and liquidations. If that business has to exist, clearly I'm glad we have a big share of it. None the less, from the point of view of the health of the economy, one would rather it wasn't necessary. There is a positive side, which is that our insolvency services are very much geared not just to the liquidation of companies but to helping them restructure and find ways round the problems. We find ourselves working with banks a great deal, and that business has been booming too.

The increased demand for insolvency services stopped our turnover from suffering as much as it otherwise would have done. That's why, out of 7,500 people, we were able to keep the number of redundancies down to 150. Even then, we worried about what some of our clients might think. But the reaction was relief that we had to run our business in the same way as they did, matching the resources available to the business in hand.

What took us by surprise was the speed at which the recession hit us. It happened very quickly as far as we're concerned. One minute we all seemed to be booming, next it was like a train hitting the buffers, as one of my partners described it. I'm also surprised by the different views one hears expressed as to whether the recession is over, and how long-lasting it has been. Personally, I don't see a great deal of recovery before the end of 1992.

Making redundancies was the biggest step we had to take, but the recession made us reflect on all our costs. We had to examine whether we got value for money for every pound we spent. That was a very productive challenge, and I wish we'd done it earlier instead of waiting for a recession.

Equally, we had to reflect on the fees we charge our clients, because they, not unnaturally, have had to ask themselves whether they are getting value for money too. We didn't reduce our rates, but we made sure we were presenting a fair bill for the job. Clearly, on occasion, you can have a slightly different view from your client about that, but we concentrated on knowing that they must get value for money. To try and persuade them that they are when they aren't is counterproductive, because you will get caught out. Any client relationship is about doing a fair job and getting paid a fair remuneration. They aren't interested in having an inexpensive job; they know professional services are not cheap. It's the quality of the service they are interested in. I'm not saying the price is irrelevant, because it isn't, but if you carry out a good job for your clients they are prepared to pay what everybody would agree was a fair price.

The main lesson to be learned from this recession is that people should never assume a period of growth will be uninterrupted. There are many people over the age of 30 who joined firms such as ours around ten years ago and assumed the boom times would be there for ever. Even people of my generation, who ought to know better. But I think we've all learnt that there will probably always be a trade cycle, so you need to be continually challenging the products and services you offer. Are they going to be needed in two years' time? In five years?

I never cease to be astounded at the propensity for some people, be they individuals or companies, to take on more and more debt, always assuming they will be able to service it and that whatever they have bought is going to increase in value. People's attitudes to house prices is a very good example. It came as a tremendous shock to find out that house prices can actually go down. But why should they always go up? It also astounds me that people can actually borrow money in such vast amounts, and clearly the banks have some responsibility for that. But it truly does amaze me that people assume there's a never-ending upward cycle, and you can borrow more and more money. There's always a come-uppance for people who manage their businesses in such an imprudent way. Many a company has been just unbelievably reckless in the push for expansion at almost any price. That is the biggest single lesson to learn. But, who knows? Another ten years of uninterrupted growth and perhaps people will fall into the same traps as before. I suspect not, actually, because the banking community has learnt some very hard lessons. Lending to Third World countries, big real estate investments in many parts of the world, and lending to speculative ventures . . . if the recession has a good side to it, that's an excellent lesson to learn.

Aside from the moral lessons, benefits from recession are difficult to find because the clear result is an enormous amount of unemployment and unhappiness. Whether a reduction in the rate of inflation is a result of the recession, or the recession is a result of a policy of having low rates of inflation is arguable. But to have a low rate of inflation is clearly a benefit, in my view. I remember reading an article in Germany which compared their house prices with ours. At the time, house prices here were going up and people regarded that as a good thing, whether they were buying or selling. In Germany, it's regarded as a bad thing. It's an interesting point to ponder on.

I'm very concerned about the continued predominance of the service economy in this country at the expense of manufacturing industry. I do sometimes wonder about a world in which nobody actually makes anything but everybody services something. I'm sad that less and less of the nation's products are actually made in this country. I don't see any sign that it will change, because more and more of our products come from the Far East. But even Hong Kong and Singapore are becoming higher cost economies than they were, and they're now managing production in other Asian countries. At the moment that trend is cascading.

Perhaps one of the biggest changes upon us is going to be the development of Europe and the establishment of the Single Market. It's going to present enormous challenges and opportunities. But a free market means that even more of our products could be manufactured in other countries. On the other hand, the establishment of a large market consisting of 320 million people – and that's without the Eastern European countries – could be a spur towards further manufacturing in Britain.

The Single Market is going to have a considerable effect on our organization. One of the driving forces behind the formation of Ernst & Young was to ensure that we could meet those challenges. As a result, we now have tremendous strength in every European country. In the last couple of years we have established new firms in Hungary, Czechoslovakia, Poland and the Commonwealth of Independent States (previously the USSR), and there are three reasons for that. We want to help major Western European businesses establish themselves in those countries; not just our existing clients, but companies we would like to have as clients. Secondly, we want to help develop our profession in these countries, where the whole concept of profit and loss has been unknown for some 40-odd years. To them, it's an entirely new concept, which is very exciting. Thirdly, by establishing our firm in each of those countries we can service the local community and attract foreign investment in the future. But we've still got a long way to go. Our resources in those four areas are only about 500-strong out of a total European workforce of 25,000.

Amongst our biggest clients we have people like Shell, BP, BTR, Hanson, British Airways, Bass and Whitbread. It's a lovely list of clients that goes on for ever and we're very grateful to have them. Equally, at the other end of the scale, our London office alone has more than 10,000 personal tax clients. There is also a group of 300 dealing with small businesses. Smaller businesses tend to require a different type of service, so it takes different skills to deal with their needs.

Big isn't necessarily beautiful. The small businessman can, on occasion, have an advantage. He doesn't have to deal with vast numbers of employees, trade unions, pension schemes and large premises. He can have a different cost structure which will enable him to compete. Clearly it depends on the products, because mass production of many products requires vast capital resources. But, depending on the product, the small businesman will always have a very important niche.

We used to think being multinational was restricted to the biggest companies only. Now it's astonishing how many comparatively small businesses are becoming multinational. These companies are looking overseas for future markets and they need a lot of help, because operating in other countries – whether in Europe or around the world – is very different. You need representation on the ground; links with local organizations, be they solicitors, accountants or bankers. That's why we've got ourselves ready; to serve those clients.

Globalization is with us, that's for sure. As the world becomes smaller, I can go to Australia on a Wednesday night and be back on the weekend. That's probably one of the disadvantages! I preferred the days when it took longer. Nowadays, communications are so fast that one does these things fairly regularly. Globalization certainly means the whole world is our market-place. Equally, it means the whole world is everybody else's market-place. It will drive us to greater efficiency because the competition is fiercer, and I believe in competition. It's hard on those who can't compete and fall by the wayside, but that's the whole ethos of a capitalist society. And we've seen in Eastern Europe that the other type of economy doesn't really work.

All British businesses should be concerned about the implications of globalization. Banks, building societies and insurance companies, for example, have to consider that in future a German savings bank will be just as free to open up in the high street. We've already seen a number of European insurance companies getting ready for the open market, so clearly there are dangers. If one doesn't recognize the competition, one is burying one's head in the sand. Of course, the world isn't going to change overnight on 1 January 1993; it will be a process of evolution. But the reality is that over the coming years, the free market will bring dangers for those who can't compete.

Strategy is an in-word these days; everybody thinks they should do some strategic planning. But if it isn't allied with a programme of how you're actually going to implement the plan, and if you don't measure that implementation against the goals you set yourselves, it's pretty useless really. I've seen quite a lot of strategic plans which have been worked on in tremendous detail end up in a drawer while people carry on as before. You need to work very, very hard at formulating corporate strategies, and you have continually to analyse the strengths of your organization. Perhaps just as important, what are its weaknesses? You need to carry out a great deal of research in order to find out what the market-place is for your service or products. There's no point in formulating corporate strategies if you don't follow them up.

I think management in the 1990s will probably end up being more professional than it was in the 1980s. In the past, there was a feeling that all it took to be a good manager was intuition. Well, you do need intuition, but a great deal of management training is also vital, certainly in a firm such as ours. It was tempting, years ago, to train people technically and then let them find their way to the top of the firm in management positions almost by accident. We now actually train our partners continuously throughout their working lives, and I think that is essential. You still need flair, but management skills can be learned.

In this country, the concept of business schools is relatively recent. At one stage, the only business schools available were firms of chartered accountants, which is one of the reasons why you see so many accountants in prominent positions in industry. While I believe that will continue, I see many more top positions in the future being filled by business school graduates. Some people say you cannot teach a forward-thinking approach by using case studies, but I think there's a lot to learn from the past. The only danger is if one assumes history repeats itself, because it doesn't. But a knowledge of history will equip you to deal with new circumstances that will happen in any environment.

To be a successful manager you have to be a good listener. You need to listen to other people's views, not necessarily before forming your own, but before finally determining your course of action. I find more and more in my career that other people's views are worth listening to, even if you discard them. I like to listen to what they have to say before making up my mind. You also need to be fair in your dealings with people. You need to be firm and decisive. Of course, taking unpleasant decisions is relatively easy compared with the more difficult task of implementing and communicating them, but you shouldn't duck any of those things.

There's no doubt that the most common management mistake is failure to appreciate the market-place. People preach a lot about service to the customer, frequently without doing anything about it. I imagine there are people who could point out to me occasions when our service to our clients regretfully hasn't been what it should. It would be nice to think in terms of 100 per cent performance but that isn't quite the real world; one can always do better. Quality is another buzz word, of course. It isn't just about the people who are out with the clients, it's about the people who man the telephone or the people who welcome you at the door as you come in. That's going to be a tremendous factor in the future. I can think of many an organization that preaches the concept of quality and service to customers without doing anything about it at all, and that's the fault of the management. You can't really expect your workforce to live and breathe the concept of quality, be it of service or product, if it doesn't come from the management.

I heard a lovely story the other day about quite a well-known German company. Their products are excellent and one of our consultants was discussing with them their quality control procedures. They pride themselves that everything leaving their factory is absolutely perfect, but in order to achieve that they throw away 15 per cent of the finished product. What a tremendous waste! Quality has to be about getting it right first time, not throwing away 15 per cent of the product when you've completed it. Think of the effect on their cost structures and, presumably, on their profits.

There was a time when we decided we really had to make our firm more market focused. Over the decades, firms such as ours had perhaps got a little bit fat. We assumed the clients would always be there and it made us a bit complacent. But we realized pretty early on that it just wasn't good enough to assume our clients would always be there because we might lose them as a result. So we really had to instil in all our people the concept of client service. You have to go out and win new business; it isn't handed to you on a plate. You have to demonstrate to your clients – and to your potential clients – why they should choose you to work for them. Instilling that into staff is quite a tough thing to do, particularly with the older generation. I give credit to my management teams for having achieved it through preaching that gospel of client service. But what delighted me was how those new concepts were actually grasped with enthusiasm by so many of our people. The will to win and beat the competition was a tremendous tonic.

The turning point in my career was when I went to work in Liberia. I was aged 30 and wasn't too sure where my future career lay. I felt I'd like to do something different for a while, so I went to work for President Tubman and led a team of people carrying out investigations for the various government departments. That job really taught me to stand on my own two feet; it established my self-confidence. I had always been a professional accountant but I discovered I actually enjoyed it. Then I went on to Germany to work for our firm in Hamburg.

Now I spend most of my life managing our firm in the UK, and I have an enormous role as one of two worldwide chairmen co-ordinating the whole of our international practice. In some ways I'm one of those people who became involved in management by accident. The biggest contribution I feel I've made in this firm is introducing people into management jobs at an age much younger than any of my predecessors would have done. I believe in the energy of youth. I have always encouraged them to grasp the opportunities that are given them and not worry about the fact that they are comparatively young.

Until fairly recently, partners in professional firms moved up the notepaper according to when they were admitted, until eventually they got to the top. Well, that didn't happen to me. I was elected to my various managing roles at an early age and I suppose there was an assumption that I might have been a bit of an exception. But I carried that through, appointing bright people who I felt could make their biggest contribution now, rather than waiting another decade. It has its dangers, because the implication to the older people is that they aren't as highly regarded in the firm as they might have thought. That is actually quite wrong, because in a professional firm such as ours I believe the most important job of all is serving clients. I have some wonderful partners in this firm who are a few years older than I am and they are the most fantastic client service partners you could ever come across. To take them away from those jobs and give them management responsibilities would be a crime. You have to make the best of people's skills. It boils down to picking the right people for management jobs regardless of their age and status in the firm.

I like to think I have an appreciation of people's problems, because we all have them. I like to think I'm sympathetic. I also like to think I'm decisive, not in any great macho way, but that I wouldn't shirk difficult issues. It's easy to give good news to people; anybody can do that. The problem is how to deliver the bad news. I try and communicate it to people in as helpful and kind a way as possible.

Sometimes I feel I could have greater powers of analysis. I can be a little bit impatient with the detail and perhaps the nitty gritty. Sometimes I feel I could be more articulate as well. But I'm aware of my weaknesses, so I tend to surround myself with people who can compensate for them. I don't do it as deliberately as that, but I believe in the power of a team, with everybody playing to everyone else's strengths. It's a mistake not to delegate, and there have been occasions when I perhaps haven't done as much of that as I should. I've probably also taken on too many things at once, with the result that on occasion I am in danger of leaving too much undone in any individual job. It's a mistake to take on a bit more than you can handle. Now and again my partners think I do, and they could just be right.

Inevitably, as our firm has got larger, one becomes a bit more remote, and that's a sadness to me. I like to say my door is always open, but these days I have so many things to do. I don't have time to walk around the corridors talking to people any more. I would prefer it if more people would just walk into my office for a chat, but that becomes increasingly difficult for people as the organization gets larger and one doesn't know them quite as well. I suppose I was quite shocked about five years ago when my then secretary told me how people thought of me. She said I was regarded as an iron fist in a velvet glove. If by that people meant I was a reasonably nice guy, but without being weak, or shirking from the tough things in life, I felt content to be seen in that way.

I do quite a lot of professional work as a member of our accounting standards board, which is very time-consuming. In an ideal world I would like to do a bit more client work. I had a non-executive directorship for a while and I enjoyed that, but I shan't do it again because I don't have the time. That really is my only regret; I don't have enough time to fulfil all my roles to my satisfaction. I'll enjoy being in Australia for a speech next Saturday afternoon. I'll go and see a client in another city on Monday and be back in my office on Tuesday. But meanwhile things have been happening here that are queueing up for me to deal with.

At the moment, I don't have any spare time for leisure activities. My wife's a keen gardener but it's noticeable that she does it all these days. I do very little. I used to play a bit of snooker and a bit of tennis, but the tennis court isn't used that much these days, and even the swimming pool, which I enjoy in the summer, doesn't get looked after as much as it did. I'm glad to say I have a very supportive wife. Supportive when she's with me and equally when I'm not there. I wouldn't say she doesn't now and again think perhaps I could be home a bit more often, but I don't really get any complaints, and that's rather important.

If I had to spend every week commuting from my home to London, it would probably drive me crazy and I would need other ways to relax. As it happens, I live out in the country and I've got a flat in London as well. I'm forever on the go somewhere, and while it may be tiring, the variety compensates for that. For instance, on a Sunday morning in the middle of winter I'll be able to walk along the beach on the Gold Coast and watch those lovely rollers come in on the Pacific. An hour's walk will do me the world of good. Recently I went to Mafeking for a couple of hours while I was in South Africa, and that was very relaxing.

I do have a fantastic job. I see an awful lot of people, because in my role as a senior partner I keep in touch with major clients. I have an enormous number of partners. I see less of them than I would like, but none the less I do see a lot of them too. I get around the country to other offices, and in my role as one of our international chairmen I am privileged to travel the world. I enjoy that. I always have to sing for my supper when I get there, of course. There's the inevitable speech when I arrive, but I enjoy that too. The variety is infinite. I am never, ever bored because I am always doing something different. I don't mean to sound self-satisfied or smug, but if I could have my time over again, there's not a lot I would change. If I could find the key to organizing my time a little better I'd do it now!

## TIPS FOR SUCCESS

- You've got to be yourself; don't try to be somebody you're not. Personalities develop naturally over a long period, but it's wrong to try and change yourself.

- Do your homework. If you haven't done the people you're dealing with the courtesy of being adequately prepared, you'll probably fall flat on your face.

- Be courageous. Deal with the bad news as well as the good.

- Be kind and sympathetic to people, even when it's hard. Having to fire somebody isn't a lot of fun, but you can still be helpful. It's an interesting test of management ability whether people still have a good view of the organization, and of you personally, when you have asked them to leave.

- Work like hell. There are no half measures; you really do have to be prepared to put in the time and commitment. After all, you've got to encourage other people to be committed, and you should never ask somebody to do something you're not prepared to do yourself.

# 4

# Jon Foulds

## *Chairman, Halifax Building Society*

*Jon Foulds is Chairman of the Halifax Building Society. Born in 1932, he served as Chief Executive of 3i Group from 1976 until 1988, when he became Non-Executive Deputy Chairman. In addition, he is a Non-Executive Director of Eurotunnel, Mercury Asset Management Group and several investment companies. He was appointed to the board of the Halifax in 1986 and became Chairman in 1990.*

It is often said that in the Stock Market, one of two passions always dominates: fear or greed. If you think you can make a bit more, then you tend to take on more, to the point where you actually over-stretch yourself.

When I first came into the City and got involved in the financing of small businesses, there was a lot of talk about companies which over-traded; that is to say they stretched their asset base too thinly for the level of business they were conducting. But in the 1970s and 1980s, as financial institutions, driven by competitive pressure, slowly abandoned their criteria, the risk profile of the business they were writing got higher almost without them realizing. I think one of the lessons to come out of this recession is that we shall see perhaps rather more orthodoxy in terms of lending in the late 1990s than we saw in the last decade.

In 1981 it was manufacturing industry that was badly hit. This time round it's the service industries, and that has obvious geographical importance because of the extent to which they are concentrated in the South East. Wearing my Halifax hat I can see the knock-on effect in terms of problems like arrears, particularly in Greater London.

This recession has probably been more severe than many commentators expected, and has also gone on for rather longer. It's tempting for the politicians and the media to talk about recovery being just around the corner, particularly in relation to the property market. But I suspect in part it's because there is a such a vested interest in reassuring everybody that their most important investment is at least likely to go up in value again, even if it's going down at the moment. It is worth noting that the current recession has been characterized – even led – by a fall in real estate values not only in the UK, but also in the US and Japan. My own view is that we are probably in an L-shaped recession. I don't fall for the idea that because the downward movement was steep and comparatively sudden the economy will bounce back just as quickly. I think we will see an improvement, but little by little.

The Halifax figures for 1991 showed a substantially increased level of arrears; certainly the highest in our history. An enormous amount of counselling has taken place within the Halifax branch network to help people with their personal budgeting and, frankly, help them to keep their homes. It's no advantage to the lender to have the upkeep of a house in possession and the risk of vandalism and so on. It's really much better to keep people in their houses even if they can't afford in the short term to meet payments in full on their mortgage. Around 40 per cent of repossessions take place because people walk into the office and give you the keys. They are people who borrowed a very high percentage of the cost of their house or flat, and now property values have fallen their homes are not worth what they paid for them. So they go and live with Granny or somebody else; find what best solution they can.

We ought not, I think, to have been surprised by what happened, following the provision in the Budget of 1989 which stopped dual mortgages carrying tax relief. The deadline was August 1989, and that produced the final flurry and froth on top of what was already an overheated market. There has been a price to pay for that, which we have all shared.

With the benefit of hindsight, we might earlier have appreciated the very significant impact that real interest rates have. Those of us who bought our houses 20 years ago enjoyed a prolonged period where we were in fact paying negative interest rates, and this has helped to create the myth that you only have to buy a house and you'll make your fortune in due course. But a house is a place to live in, primarily, and it should be seen as an investment only secondarily.

The Halifax never changed its lending standards, even at the peak of the boom. But early on we switched the emphasis in our lending, and in the design of our savings products, to go for what we considered to be the best part of the market. In other words, we redefined the market and quite consciously lost market share in order to preserve asset quality. We might have done that a little earlier, and we might have reinforced some of the discipline on lending a little earlier than we did, but broadly speaking I think the Halifax comes out of it well.

On the basis of any industry comparison, our expense ratios have been very significantly lower than many building societies – not all, but many – and certainly significantly lower than the clearing banks. So it hasn't actually been necessary for us to take management action in terms of redundancies. In fact, we've had no redundancies in the building society caused by the recession, I'm glad to say. But we have consciously adopted a cautious lending policy, and taken action to improve the quality of our underwriting, the strength of our administration and the discipline that's essential if you're to write a sound mortgage book.

It's always easy to blame the banks and the building societies when things go wrong, but these organizations only stimulate markets up to a point. The responsibility for creating the climate in which business is carried out is that of the government, and I think the policy which was followed of using interest rates as the sole weapon against inflation was mistaken. Those of us who stand in the market-place respond to the conditions created by government. There certainly have been some lenders who have done and possibly still are doing silly things. Following deregulation – or perhaps one should say re-regulation – the spreads in banking were driven down to levels which I would say were uneconomic. One sees the banks being pilloried for the way in which they have treated small customers, and for taking advantage of the circumstances in order to drive up interest margins, but those margins are not at the level they were some years ago. The fact is, if you charge a very low level of margin, you don't build the profits which enable you to take risks in terms of your lending. So the lower the margins, the more conservative your lending has to be. If one is thinking in terms of stimulating the economy, then arguably the banks ought to be allowed to increase their profits, because they will then be less risk-averse.

Wearing my venture capital hat, the category of business where the level of lending was highest during the boom was the management buy-out. But it always struck me as odd that in many financial institutions there were people sitting at adjoining desks with com-pletely different attitudes. At one desk, they were arguing with companies who wished to increase the borrowing level under an old debenture document to perhaps twice the net asset value, and charging an additional percentage for giving their consent. At the next desk, another investor would be looking avidly at a management buy-out opportunity where he would be sharing in a level of debt which was perhaps five times the shareholders' funds.

In the early days of management buy-outs many people did well, partly because economic conditions were better, which meant asset disposals were more easily achieved. But once you get into a recession, asset disposals – if they can be achieved at all – only happen at lower prices. And the burden of a very high level of debt when the government is relying on high interest rates to control the economy can be a killer.

Going back a long time to when I first joined the company that was then called ICFC, I remember being struck by the difference in attitudes between those who had run companies in the latter part of the 1930s and those who had come into business after the Second World War and hadn't experienced those earlier difficult years.

This time round, the businessmen who had run their companies through the 1981 recession thought first of all in terms of operating within a limited cash pool, and anything which could preserve cash had to be done. Perhaps that experience – and the increased efficiencies that came out of it – has helped those businesses to weather this recession more readily than they might otherwise have done. Every cloud is said to have a silver lining, though sometimes it is difficult to discern. But businesses that survive recessions do emerge fitter, leaner and more cost-conscious.

The managers who have lived through two recessions in the last ten years will become more conservative, certainly in terms of the exposure to risk that they will readily accept. In addition, today's managers are more open-minded to technology and to change. In both those important respects, the 1990s managers are probably better than many of their predecessors.

A successful manager is one with the ability to stimulate and manage change, and in the financial services sector over the last ten years we've seen an almost unprecedented level of change. One of my pet theories is that all businesses have a threshold of change, and you push beyond that threshold at your peril. Those businesses which experience the highest levels of change actually develop a tolerance to it. They become the businesses which find change the easiest to accept. We've got lots of examples in the post-war period – I am thinking particularly of the engineering and textile industries – where there was an inadequate appreciation of the implications of changes in technology, a reluctance to accept new working practices and a reluctance to invest. In the end, those businesses fail.

During the fat years, all companies, to a greater or lesser extent, create excesses which in bad times must absolutely be cut out. That includes, inevitably, over-manning; sometimes as a result of casual management and sometimes in anticipation of increasing the size of the business which is then frustrated by economic conditions. Redundancy is always a very unpleasant business; not only for the people who have to find new jobs, but also for the rest of the organization. People feel unsettled and vulnerable. If you have to make redundancies, you ought to make sure you clean out the stable in one go. Otherwise, if the exercise happens repeatedly, the organization feels it is dying the death of a thousand cuts. Morale drops, which makes management much more difficult. So if you've got to do it, put the knife in deep, rather than trying to be kind to protect something which, in the long run, you cannot protect adequately. I suppose, by definition, a crisis means a circumstance which one had not anticipated. So one should pause later and wonder why one didn't anticipate this event, and look at the weaknesses exposed within the business, perhaps in the planning function, or operationally. But the first thing to do is to keep your cool. Think carefully, and act resolutely.

Recessions do end, and perhaps the most common management mistake is to allow one's time horizon to shrink. The upturn does come, so to cut back too much on marketing, or to cut back on research and development where the time frame may be ten years . . . those are mistakes I would try to avoid. One tries to be in a position as the recession ends – and in this case I see that as a very gradual process – where the machine is ready to accelerate. One should try to have the right people, adequately trained, and supported by the right investment, to build on the entity one has had to cut back to.

Small businesses, by definition, are not global. There are very few brands that are really global. Coca Cola is an obvious one, but there aren't many. Within an economy as big as the United States, there is not really one market-place. It's more like 12 market-places, with local brands often operating very successfully in each. A global business has a whole raft of different kinds of management problems. Even a company which might have ambitions to become a pan-European business is going to have to change the way in which it thinks about management succession, for example. You will never recruit top people in countries away from your domestic market unless those people believe they have an equal chance of running the whole business in the future. There's a cultural change implied in that which in practice is extremely difficult to get to grips with. There are American companies run by Brits, but not many. They're mostly run by Americans. French companies operating nationally tend to be run by Frenchmen, and so on. But I believe if you want to have an international strategy, you have to offer equal opportunities.

At 3i we expanded the business outside the UK, principally into continental Europe, but also into the United States in a smaller way. We have gained advantage from the geographical diversification, because the recession in those continental European countries hasn't yet been as marked as it has here. So we've been able to develop those businesses at a relatively fast rate; it's been a defensive strength.

I was interested at 3i in the problems of hi-tech companies in the UK. One is typically dealing with technology which has a very limited life in market terms because it's likely to be superseded by the second-generation product very quickly. It was, in practice, very difficult for these companies to expand into Europe, for linguistic reasons, for cultural reasons . . . for the simple difficulty of transferring goods across national boundaries. Things which ultimately will happen quite naturally with the Single Market. For those businesses producing hi-tech products, which potentially have a world market, the natural basis of expansion should be Europe. In fact, because Europe was a multiplicity of markets, many people turned to the United States, where there was a much easier acceptance of hi-tech, and where the market-place was almost as large as the whole of Europe combined.

America looked very seductive for people who were in the hi-tech business, but not all of them succeeded. Many people came unstuck; mostly because they didn't do their groundwork thoroughly, or felt unable to delegate sufficiently to local management. A few years ago there were two great attractions to the United States. One was that they spoke a language which we could understand, and the other was that at a time when socialism was gaining ground in Europe, they were playing the game by rules which people believed they understood.

Personally, I am a convinced European. For some years the fastest growth in exports from the UK has been to other EC countries. Had we not been a member of the EC our economy would have been in a significantly worse state than it is. It's difficult not to be an enthusiast about the EC if you're a businessman, and at the time of the referendum on Europe, the business community came out very solidly in favour.

The prime job of business is to make money for the shareholders, but beyond that narrow definition one has to recognize a responsibility to employees, to suppliers, and to the communities in which one works. And there are some delicate balances to be struck involving ecological considerations. Capitalism in the 20th century is more enlightened than the capitalism of the 19th century. I don't see capitalism as a fixed philosophy; I see it as an evolutionary one in which, to take a small example, reinforcing the work of employees interested in charitable activities is just one part of being a responsible member of the community.

Companies should, I suggest, take a broad view of what constitutes self-interest, because a lot of things people talk about as being for the common good are no more than taking a view of what in the long term is in one's own interest. Take the example of a business which is a major employer in a provincial town. It should have a keen interest in things like local education, because that is the pool from which the future labour resource will come.

One turning point in my career came a long time ago. I started my working life in the family textile business in Lancashire; that was a pretty hard school. I recommended to the family that we should close it down. So my first experience in business was in recession, and I think that left a mark on me. It certainly made me reflect on what I wanted to do subsequently. I made a conscious decision that I would either go into property or something to do with money, on the basis that those two commodities were the common denominator of all business activity. If I was skilled in either then I could probably hold my own.

Perhaps my mistake was not to have gone into property; I would have been a great deal richer than I am now. I'm quite proud of having been chief executive of 3i for almost 12 years, during which the business expanded enormously. I was lucky to do that through what now looks like 'The golden 1980s'; in a sense, the tide of history was with me. But within that period I am pleased I was able to turn an organization which was sales driven into one which adopted a marketing philosophy in the full sense of the term.

During my time at 3i I possibly brought rather more imagination than might have been there otherwise. I had a dealing instinct, but nevertheless acquired an interest in management, so I was able to see more than one side of the problems we had. Many of those problems were the problems of success, apart from that difficult period in 1980–81. It took much longer to come out of that recession than we thought it would at the time.

One of the lessons we learned was that while companies contract within a given cash supply during a period of recession, many of the failures come as the economy takes off and the cash requirements grow with it. They run out of road because they over-trade, and their financial controls aren't good enough. Our experience over many, many years was that companies which fail do so either as a result of weakness in financial controls or poor marketing. They don't often fail because they have a lousy product; at least, they don't fail overnight. But if they don't understand about cash management, or they can't find a market for their goods, then they fail very quickly. And I think in this recession that is as true as it was in 1980–81.

Some people in comparable positions have a much higher public profile than me. If one isn't careful, the media – and I use that term very generally – can make demands. I've never wanted to be a public personality, so I haven't sought the circumstances where that can happen. The satisfaction in my role comes partly from believing that one can contribute, either from one's experience or native wit. You actually have to offer something which helps to improve the performance of the people you are working with. Satisfaction also comes from always continuing to learn, and from feeling that one is pushing oneself to the limit of whatever ability one possesses.

One of my weaknesses is that I don't like detail very much. Another is that I tend to be impatient; I can't understand why people won't get on with things once a decision has been made. With that impatient side I sometimes miss some of the more profound aspects of what I am supposed to be doing. I also have a very low boredom threshold!

A lot of people in business, including me, get intensely interested in what they're doing to the point where they exclude themselves from things which in the long run would make them more interesting human beings. To relax, in part I play sport. I love skiing; I love playing tennis. I read a bit, but I find that by the time I've read all the papers associated with the various things I'm involved with, I don't read as much literature as I would like. I enjoy going to the cinema, I enjoy going to look at pictures ... I buy a picture occasionally. It all fills the time abundantly.

I think it's possible to be successful with or without a family. It's certainly very much more agreeable to do it with one, but a successful business life does impose stresses, and one has got to be lucky enough to have somebody who understands why those stresses are important. Not in terms of earning a living, but in terms of how one feels about one's personal development. Certainly a secure family life is a great anchor.

During the years I spent working full time at 3i, I looked forward to Monday mornings as soon as it got to Friday night. There were very few periods – and all of them short – when I did anything other than look forward to going into the office. In that respect, I've been extremely lucky. If I had my time over again, I would be very fortunate to be as exposed to the variety of situations, the quality of human beings and the general interest that I have had in my business life. But if I was to have one thought, it might be to wonder seriously about whether I shouldn't have gone into business on my own.

## TIPS FOR SUCCESS

- Work hard. Working hard actually does produce its own reward.

- How you define work is another matter, but if you want to be successful in business, it's not enough to work hard: you've actually got to be there. Somebody once said to me the first thing you're paid for is to be there, and there's a lot of truth in that. If you're away too much, you may come back and find your desk in the hall. At a certain stage in one's career it means one really can't afford to take on a great number of outside interests, whether charitable, local sports clubs or whatever. You have to have a very high degree of commitment.

- You've got to be lucky. Perhaps by that I mean you have got to condition yourself by aptitude and by circumstances to recognize an opportunity when you see one. In other words, largely – but not entirely – you get the luck you deserve.

- You will be best at doing things you enjoy. I don't think one can force oneself into the mode of being a chartered accountant, which I am not, if one is naturally ill at ease with numbers.

• You have to follow your own star; be your own person. However improbable the direction in which that takes you, the chances are that in the long run, if you follow it, you will be a success. And I don't necessarily just mean a success financially, I mean in personal terms.

# 5

# Sir Owen Green

## *Chairman, BTR*

*Sir Owen Green is Chairman of BTR, one of British engineering's most successful multinational companies. He was born in 1925 and qualified as a chartered accountant following Royal Naval war service. In 1956 he was appointed Financial Director of Oil Feed Engineering, which was later acquired by BTR. After holding a number of positions in BTR's field operations, he became Managing Director in 1967, and Chairman and Chief Executive in 1984. Sir Owen's success in turning a small rubber company into a highly profitable international group is unparalleled in British industry.*

The 1980s was a funny period. Frankly, I don't think management in the 1980s had to be anything like as good as it had to be in the 1970s, or as it is going to have to be in the 1990s. It really wasn't difficult for managers for much of the 1980s. There were bull markets everywhere, and it's not difficult to manage in those situations.

But the real business world of today is pretty tough, and the best way I could describe going through this recession is the description that the Duke of Wellington used during the Peninsular War: 'hard pounding', that's what gets you through. Never giving up, just sticking in there and doing what you have to do. You never, ever, relent, and you never relax your vigilance. I think this is what the 1990s are going to be about: 'hard pounding'.

It seems to me that this has been a true world recession. All the economies have been affected, which in my experience is unusual. In fact, I think later when we look back in the history books, they'll probably say it was a depression, rather than a recession. In the 1980s the world was living off the fat, and really wasn't producing. But I don't think we realized the extent to which the 1980s would have to be paid for. We didn't expect the geographical extent of the correction; we didn't expect the whole world to go into reverse. And at BTR, we thought we were recession resistant to a greater extent than has proved to be the case.

After 23 years of successive increases in profit, we've had our first setback; it's been that bad. We didn't run round like chickens with their heads off, but naturally as the business continued to decline, we had to cut costs. Unfortunately, when you cut costs, you have to start with people, because people generate costs. It isn't just a question of the salaries, it's the overheads that go with them. When you employ people, you employ substantial overheads, and in order to get those down, frankly, you've got to cut people too.

So one of the things we had to do, sadly, was bring down our number of employees in relation to the business that was available. In 1990 we had about 10,000 redundancies; in 1991 we had a further 5,000, which is between 10 and 15 per cent of our total population of employees, and accorded with the level of market decline. But making redundancies produces an imbalance of its own. For example, there is a minimum level at which an operating unit can perform, and if you go below that level then you have to be prepared either to sit and lose money for an indeterminate period, or to close that particular unit down or fold back into another operation if you can.

In retrospect, we should have taken out people earlier, but I've been through three recessions now and I think we'll make the same mistake next time. There's a tremendous psychological problem, because the managers who have to make redundancies are very close to their employees. It's all right saying you need a 5 per cent reduction when you're up in an ivory tower, but to implement it meets with a lot of resistance. To use a military analogy, it's rather like needing to have different types of Generals. Some Generals are great at attacking, others are great at defending. But unfortunately, in our business, you can't keep chopping and changing Generals, so we didn't, and don't, act quickly enough in reducing people.

Another reason is that when a downturn comes along we're always hoping it's only going to last three months. Then it goes on for six, and we begin to believe we're in recession, so by the time we dive in there we're at least three months behind the score. The lesson to be learned, I suppose, is that as soon as the writing is on the wall you should read it. You should steel yourself to take the necessary action. If I was a manager, as I was years ago, then next time round I think I would take the view that it was going to be bad, rather than hope that it wasn't.

Companies which maintained their advertising budgets in order to increase their share of the market were throwing money down the drain. People always worry that when the recovery comes, if they're not ready, it'll pass them by. But you should assume that your competitor is in the same boat, because he is! Therefore you should accept that you may have to sacrifice – but you probably won't – some of the rapid growth when the economy moves up. As Roosevelt said, you have nothing to fear but fear itself. Everybody tells me this economy's going to move up very slowly, in which case you won't have to sacrifice anything. I'm saying take the chance: meet things as they come. Act, and manage, in real time.

In military terms, during recession you retreat. You withdraw into the boundaries of your costs. All the time, you're trying to cut your coat according to the cloth that is available. The most important thing all companies have to do in recession is watch the cash. If you're a very small company, everything else has to go by the board because you're inevitably going to be in the hands of your bankers, and bankers are not always understanding. They can't afford to be.

So as a small company, you literally have to just manage for cash. Any big ideas, any forward plans, have to be trimmed, because you're managing for survival, which means cash. Larger companies don't have quite the same problem, but they still have to watch their gearing. They have to be sure that at any time they are able to meet the requirements of their bankers, who are pretty objective task masters. I wouldn't be one to condemn the banks. They give out a lot of rope, but if they see that the thing on the end of the rope isn't responding, then of course they pull in.

Bankers are in a very competitive industry. Their business is to buy and sell finance. Frankly, the international banking community, and the governments of the world, set a very bad example in the 1980s. They advanced far too much money to the Third World; it almost got to the stage where they were competing to throw money down a drain. It became the fashion. In the world of commerce, they were lending money pretty loosely, too. Meanwhile, the merchant banks encouraged this whole concept of junk financing, of management buy-outs. That level of financing could only have made sense if there was not even a hiccup in the world economies from then on.

So from 1984, particularly in the US, but also in the UK, we had these tremendous buy-outs which were absolutely dependent on the economies continuing to grow. The gearing of these buy-outs was such that you could have 95 per cent loan and 5 per cent equity. Now that's fine, providing economies do keep on growing, but as soon as the world slows up and it's difficult to get money, they have to push up the interest rates in order to attract the money. And that's when you get what I call a double whammy. The effect of a recession combined with an increase in interest rates has been absolutely devastating on these over-geared companies. Yes, the banks were to blame; but only in the broadest sense. The people who got themselves into these circumstances were also very much to blame. These so-called entrepreneurs; they were stupid. They thought they were clever, but they weren't.

I don't actually think there has been that much diversification. Seven or eight years ago this expression 'focusing' came in. It became fashionable to talk about reducing diversification. That was already in before the recession, so I don't think the problem was diversification so much as hubris. There was a hell of a lot of hubris in every direction. In the early 1980s, the media introduced league tables for everybody, even accountants, to show who was the biggest, and that fed the egos of the players. It was a very frothy business environment. If I had my way, there'd never be another league table again.

When I started in business after the war, the big management consultants of the time based their advice on what had been right for military purposes, so you had very strong organization structures. BTR broke away from it in the 1960s, but most large companies didn't, and it was only in the 1980s that they began to do what they should have done 20 years earlier. Society has moved on, and politics, industry and commerce have reflected that change. The whole activity has moved away from the rigidity of central control. People are fed up with bureaucracy, and it is a world phenomenon that central control economies – and companies – are a thing of the past. The best example, of course, is what's happened in the USSR (now the Commonwealth of Independent States).

I'm not a great Common Market fan. I don't think that big is beautiful, and I would say that there is going to be tremendous scope for small companies in regional and national markets. The Single Market isn't going to change that, whatever anybody says. You've only got to look at the US to see that. The US is the largest single economy in the world: 250 million people speaking one tongue, obeying one federal law. The whole thing is an example to the rest of the world of a beautiful economy, despite balance of payments questions. But when you get into the US, you realize it's no more one economy than the houses in one street. So many people have come unstuck by saying 'We're going to put down our flag in the US.' Fatal. The first thing they've got to do is put down their flag in New York State, or Texas, or California, and start from there. If you want to cover the US, you need to have distribution units in almost every city of every state, and you have to have your manufacturing units close by. There are 47 geographically economic areas in the US, and the majority of companies in each will be serving those economies. They'll be doing wonderfully; relatively few companies in number will be national. The same applies with the global economy. It's very important and very lucrative for big players, but most of the free world's enterprises will be local. Not even national; they'll be regional.

So I don't think things will change that much. I think the big will get bigger, but I'm not saying the small will get smaller. There'll be a tremendous market for them, and I wouldn't wish to encourage the majority of the smaller companies, who are doing quite well in their own way, to have global aspirations.

Italy is a very interesting example. Italy is a country that has always been broke. Nobody understands how it works; it's got about 15 economies. In a way, it's a bit like the US only smaller, and you get this tremendous interplay of businesses on a regional basis. So if you're in Naples, small businesses trade with each other. One makes buttons, one makes thread, another one makes clothes, and occasionally they may have a little trading with Lombardy or Piedmont. Of course, there are global and national companies like Fiat, and the big Italian state corporations. But the well-being of the economy depends on these small, regional operations. They just carry on trading while the nation goes broke, and few pay any taxes. Rome is ignored, and everyone enjoys themselves. They have quite a high standard of living. Many other countries operate like that, so I don't think companies should really go overboard on the global concept unless they really are large, world players.

I'm not really worried about competition from abroad. We've had a lot of competition from the Germans in certain parts of our business over the last 30 years, but we've never regarded them as serious competition in the UK, and I see no reason to regard them as that now. Similarly, we've been in Germany for 30 years. We'd like to think we've been effective competition, but have we?

What we do globally is to ensure that our managers are locals. The Americans have always been weaker in their overseas activities; they're not very good at global expansion because they don't know how to use the locals. The Americans will have vice-presidents for every country in the world sitting in a tower block in New York. None of them wants to go abroad because they don't want to lose their position in the hierarchy, so they stay at home. The British have always been better at 'colonialism', at exploiting overseas, because we have been prepared to work through locals. Recognition of nationalism, of regional preferences and so on, is very important.

When it comes to forming corporate strategies, the emphasis should be on decentralization. Autonomy has got to be local. Decisions should be made as near as possible to the place where the decision is required. As the world speeds up, perhaps we will have more competition. I don't think we will; I think there will be less. But if there is to be more competition, then decisiveness is very important. There has to be more power passed down. You have to allow mistakes to be made – local managers have to suffer them – but you also have to find a way of controlling the size of the mistakes.

I think there will still be expansion throughout the 1990s, but the development of our ability to reproduce an article precisely, cheaply and repetitively is going to have a dramatic effect. The need for large manufacturing centres is disappearing. You can go into a basement in Japan and there will be a £100,000 piece of equipment sitting there churning out complex materials. It won't even be managed by one person. Someone may come and check it every three or four hours – maybe the wife upstairs – so the whole issue of cheap labour will disappear, because labour isn't going to be terribly important. The whole question of skill will substantially disappear too, because the skill is in the equipment itself. Automation could really affect all this thinking about single markets, and the way in which these markets are tackled, quite profoundly. The UK might again become a wool and textiles and metal-forming country.

The recession had to happen, and it's been the first real challenge for our younger managers. If it hadn't happened, it would need to have been invented. Business schools can't teach you about recession; you've got to live through it. And there's no doubt in my mind that since a recession is going to happen every so often, our younger managers have had a very useful experience. It's been unavoidably painful, but the younger they are the less painful it is because they're more resilient.

But having eliminated all the froth of the 1980s, are we back where we were, or have we moved on from there? I do think there is greater equality in the way in which people are regarded. Certainly in the UK, there's no doubt about that. It's made quite a difference to labour relations, trade unions and management, so we have moved on in some areas; in terms of respect for the individual.

Where I don't think we've moved on at all is in respect for work. And that is the basic problem: people don't respect that which occupies most of their lives. It's a thing called work, but we should invent another word for it because it ought to be a pleasure. It's worse now than it was in the 1960s and 1970s; it's become even more of a drudge. People work to earn enough to let them live as they want to live. They're not interested in this thing called work. They want to do other things which they call play. We see it now in that country which is held up as a paragon of work respect: Germany. The highest absenteeism problem we have is in our German operations; it can be more than 20 per cent. They've got the same disease. You might say that's a good thing, because their competitiveness is going to reduce. But I think it's sad for Western society that the more we develop, the less we have regard for this wonderful experience – this exciting, sharpening, blood-coursing activity – called work.

I wouldn't say we'll never go back to the frothy 1980s, because when memories have dimmed, mankind will be back to its old tricks. You know that expression 'There's one born every minute'? Well, there's a sucker who's going to come along in 15 to 20 years' time, or even less than that – as soon as memories have been allowed to dim – then we'll have the same thing all over again.

To be a successful manager, you have to have average intelligence (you don't need great intelligence), common sense, and an inquiring mind. You have to be a fairly stable sort of person, but not too stable. The trouble with common sense is that it's very uncommon. But I've never met a manager yet who I would regard as a complete manager who did not have an inquiring mind. It's exploring the unknown, finding new frontiers, broadening your life. That particular characteristic which I call an inquiring mind is very essential.

Learning how to get the best out of people is part of common sense, but I don't think it's the most important aspect of a manager's job. Because included in management is leadership, and I don't think you're necessarily leading when you're concentrating on just getting the best out of people. Setting standards by example is very important, and that's the way I believe you get the best out of people, rather than through a psychological study of each person's mind. Leadership is what most people are looking for. I've always said to our people, don't look for the pips on the shoulder, the stripes on the arm, because the title doesn't make that person the leader. You just look for somebody you respect; somebody you regard as the leader. That's the person really to follow.

I discovered many years ago in the Navy that in war, the mass recognizes leadership by behaviour, not by title and rank. As far as society's concerned, I think we miss National Service. Discipline hones people's minds towards reacting not in an automatic way, but in a sensible way. The family used to practise it: some parents were good and some were bad, but perversely enough, the thing that caused discipline to disappear was a war, and reaction to it. I would be very happy if within the family we could restore that type of respect that doesn't seem to exist now, because as a result there's no self-motivation.

I'm a great believer in family life. Having said that, my children would say that when they were growing up they hardly saw me; I wasn't around. But I really do feel that a family unit is very important. It helps you become a complete person. Loyalty is very important in a family. It's important in business life too. Many people believe that loyalty has to come up from below. I've never asked people beneath me for loyalty, but I've always given it.

As a manager, you don't have time to study each employee individually, but you do need to develop an attitude of recognition. The Americans have it jolly well; they know all the Christian names and they walk around the factory, talking to Joe and slapping Jim on the back. As soon as they go home, they may have forgotten all about them, but it doesn't matter. I say to our people, just as often as you give someone a pat on the back or praise them for doing something, don't be afraid to scold them if necessary. Scolding is an act of recognition, and an individual appreciates that. When you need to fire someone, the worst thing is failing to do it. If a person judges that he is not really doing the job and is scared of being fired, and the manager is rather reluctant to fire him, you go through this uncomfortable apprehensive period. Almost without fail, when it comes to the parting of the ways, the individual concerned is relieved that it's over. Recognition - identifying, communicating and dealing with the issues, whether they're good or bad – is very important.

We don't have 'mission statements' at BTR, and we never have had them. When you think about it, all these words are 'nothings'. They're just PR words. You get all these 'isms' . . . it's the management consultants who start them off, and words keep being added to the vocabulary. I don't believe too much in 'focus'; I call it hocus pocus. In the 1970s they introduced 'corporate culture'. Everybody had to have one. And in the middle of the 1980s, that became 'the mission statement'. We have 'core business' – that which

is left after the apple has been eaten! I don't think it does anything
for the ordinary employee. I don't think it means anything to him at
all. It's a business school thing: let's talk about corporate culture, let's
have our goals and mission statements and so on. But the man on the
shop floor doesn't see it that way. He's working in real time; he's
flesh and blood, he's thinking and talking about his own aspirations.

The turning point in my life was when I decided in 1954 to move
from a professional career as an auditor into industry as a manager.
I discovered I was inadequately fulfilled as a financial adviser,
because I was giving advice which could be accepted or rejected. Even
if it was accepted, it wasn't terribly fulfilling unless you were satisfied
with being once-removed from the action. I needed to become
involved in the decision-taking process, and in the implementation
of those decisions.

But what taught me more than anything, and gave me more
experience than I've ever had since in my life, was being in the Navy
at the age of 18. I've never again had the responsibility in my career
that I had at that age: the life and death of people. When I came into
Civvy Street, I realized there weren't any decisions which were that
important, that significant, or that profound. Something like that puts
everything into perspective, and it has always stayed with me. People
sometimes say that I carry responsibility well. If so, it's because I've
never had as much responsibility as I had in my youth.

People have an image of me: it's always overblown, of course.
Leader, strongly opinionated, great power, very modest. Miserable,
cheese paring, runs a tight ship . . . all those things. Well, I've always
found it very difficult deliberately to waste money, to spend it
without feeling that I'd assessed the potential value of that spend.
That's why I never would have been any good in an entirely
consumer business: wines and spirits, high fashion, that sort of thing.
I wouldn't have been able to bring myself to make the big decisions
that these people make on the type of information available to them.
You make money out of it, of course, if you're clever. But I think
you have to be lucky too. I am, I suppose, cautious in that respect,
and careful about the way in which our company has spent money,
which I think is a strength.

I've always cared very much about people, though not with a
bleeding heart. I've always recognized the importance of managers,
and I always try to talk to people. Formerly I used to speak to
managers weekly, but we grew too big for that, so just occasionally
I'll ring a manager and talk about his business and the world in

general. I'm interested in what motivates people. In the business game, you have to be. I've always had an inquiring mind. I've always wanted to know why, not so much mechanically how, but why something works. I've always said there's nothing new under the sun; many things which are presented as inventions, or as new concepts, are the products of lateral thinking. It's analogy. And I've encouraged our people to think in analogous terms.

Anybody can be an innovator. The office boy can be an innovator. I remember reading about the Swiss gentleman who invented Velcro after he got those burrs sticking to him from the hedgerows. If you see a phenomenon, and you can translate it to another application, you can be thought of as being brilliant and original. I've always tried to stimulate our people in a modest way to do that sort of thing. But there's little really original in my view.

I've always been able to delegate, because the ego thing has never been a problem for me at all. In fact, people might say that I delegate too much. That hasn't necessarily been seen by the market.

The market talks about 'my' company, and it has always irritated me. There were four or five people who built up this business, all of whom have now retired or moved in other directions. It was a team effort, and I feel it's very inappropriate to trivialize companies in the way that the media often do.

I must have a lot of weaknesses, because it's a human condition, but as long as the strengths outweigh the weaknesses, I suppose it's all right. And when you're aware of these tendencies, it's easier to do something about them. I could be just a little bit too people-conscious . . . I may be too concerned. That can be a weakness, particularly in the top man. I can't say I've ever been let down by people, but perhaps it has occupied a bit more of my time than it should have done. I think about people in my own personal, private time, when I might have been thinking of other things.

Work has never been stressful for me – I find it relaxing – but when I get time, I play a bit of golf. I've played for 30 or 40 years, and I really do play it badly. I don't have a handicap; I just go out there and hit the ball. You know one of the reasons I took it up? Because if there was to have been any excess of ego, then a round on the golf course will find that out. Unless you're a very good player, you're just one of the crowd. You can't blame anybody for your mistakes on the golf course. If you slice a ball, it's down to you. Golf is sort of humbling; it certainly keeps your feet on the ground. It also tells you something about other people. It's very easy to cheat at golf, and when a big man does it, you've got to say there's a weakness there. Golf is a sport that brings out certain frailties in the human condition. I like to think that because I persevere, it means something. Maybe tenacity.

## TIPS FOR SUCCESS

- You must have an inquiring mind. Be an innovator. Become a leader, and develop an attitude of recognition. Like people, even if it is a weakness.

- As soon as the writing is there on the wall, read it, and take the necessary action. Manage in real time.

- Delegate. Make sure decision-making takes place locally.

- Don't go overboard on the global concept. There is going to be tremendous scope for small companies in regional and national markets.

- Don't forget the lessons of this recession. And never assume interest rates aren't going to rise.

# 6

# Peter Gummer

## *Chairman, Shandwick*

*Peter Gummer is Chairman of Shandwick, the largest public relations group in the world. He was educated at Selwyn College, Cambridge, and after working on local newspapers held a number of public relations posts before forming Shandwick in 1974. The company now employs approximately 1,800 people in 50 offices around the world, and has fees in excess of £100m.*

Politicians and economists expect this recession to follow the pattern of history, but the world is structurally different now. We're much more dependent on what is happening in other parts of the globe, both economically and politically, and that affects the way we carry out our business.

Jet-lagged at 3am in November 1991, I was watching an interview on CNN which confirmed in my mind that America was going deeper into recession. So I went to America and became even more convinced. 'Double-dip' may prove to be wrong, but there is not going to be a quick recovery in 1992, I have no doubt about that. And if America doesn't recover, that is going to slow up recovery in the UK.

People are beginning to see that not only was 1991 bad, 1992 may be equally dangerous. There are major problems with the German economy, big problems in France, and in Tokyo there is a genuine feeling that people want to go backwards into Japan, rather than push outwards as they have in recent years and invest in America and Europe. I don't see a real recovery coming until 1993, and it is interesting to note that the Organization for Economic Co-operation and Development (OECD) has revised its 1992 growth forecasts for the 24 economies in the organization from 2.9 to 2.2 per cent. The downgrading of the growth outlook reflects weaknesses in America and slow-downs in Germany and Japan.

So in November I decided that if I felt this badly about tomorrow, I should do something about it. Shandwick had a reasonably good 15 month period to the end of October 1991 in terms of fees: around £120m, which is about the same as the previous year. I said to myself that if 1992 is going to be so difficult, we ought to look at the worst level of fees that it could bring and assume there will be no new international business and no referrals. Just taking the business we have inside the operations already, we decided that we would probably earn about £100m in 1992, so we then structured our costs accordingly, based on almost nil growth.

The result is that I re-organized the entire business worldwide, incurring millions in redundancy and rationalization costs. There were 300 redundancies, which is about 15 per cent of the workforce. The rest of it related to potential business. We carry, perfectly properly, in our books, an element of 'work in progress' for business which is under negotiation, of which there is quite a lot. In the half year, for example, we had about £60m of international fees from 50 clients under negotiation. Although some of that business still looks as though it might come on stream, I am so pessimistic about 1992 that I wrote off all the work in progress last year and all the associated costs. This put a very clean edge against 31 October 1991, with all the bad news behind us, but obviously it was a shattering experience for the staff, the clients and the shareholders.

In reality, we had a cost structure which was quite inappropriate to the circumstances in which we found ourselves. No more acquisitions, no more double-digit organic growth. . . . at least for a year or two. It showed so clearly that in business you must be both realistic and resilient. If you believe things are getting worse, it's no good saying 'I hope they're going to get better'. You've got to do something about it, and you've got to be prepared, having taken the action that flows from being realistic, to get up and battle your point home. If people don't accept it, you just have to say to yourself 'Well, that's life.' But you must be resilient and appear positive in all that you do.

Sometimes little things happen over the period between the birth of an idea and the conclusion of it which change the way you view it. Three things happened to me.

The first was when I read Sir Owen Green's chapter during the preparation of this book. I thought it was a brilliant exposition of exactly the problems I am talking about. Afterwards I wrote him a little note to say that I was taking some very heavy decisions, and I wanted him to know that reading the clarity of what he had said gave me more strength to do it than I otherwise would have had.

The second was reading Ivan Fallon's book on Jimmy Goldsmith called *Billionaire* (Hutchinson, 1991). In one paragraph he says Goldsmith recognizes upturns and downswings before the market does, which is what is unnerving about him. He plays his hand behind what he sees, and that is essential. When I read it, I said to myself 'That's exactly what I must do. If I feel so strongly about what is going on in our particular market-place then we must do something about it.'

Then one night I was sitting in the bath and Lucy, my wife, came to talk to me. She said 'I've only got one question. What happens if, after taking all these decisions, you're wrong?' So I thought for a minute, and I said 'Well, we're a better business if I'm wrong, because everything I have done has been so thorough that I feel enormously confident the business is stronger and fitter as a result.'

I took that thought with me the next day when I went to see the chief executive of Lloyds bank. I told him what I was doing, and said I was very worried about the implications; the terrible press I was going to get, the loss of pride, and so on. But he thought I was absolutely right in my prognosis for 1992. He said the most difficult thing about what I was doing was making the very last cut, that last million or two. And he said 'When you feel yourself resisting that last little bit, do it, because if you don't get it all done in one go you will have a shadow hanging over your '92 or '93 figures.' I thought that was a very wise piece of counsel.

We have a very skilled gardener in the country, and when he's pruned the roses and we're down to those tiny little bits with hardly anything on them, I say to him 'Gosh, Randal, I think you've killed them.' He pats me gently on the head and disappears with a grunt, but it's hard to believe that these tiny little things will develop into beautiful blooms in so few months. That is what it feels like with a business: you say to yourself 'Will it really blossom again if I cut that huge great bit off there?'

I talked to a lot of senior business friends beforehand and asked their opinions. Not one person said 'Peter, you've gone off your rocker.' I had a terrible weekend of last minute wobbles before we made our actions public, and on the Monday we had a board meeting and discussed the whole thing yet again. Having non-executive directors to whom you can talk, and who have no axe to grind, is a great strength.

On D-day we rang all the companies in the group, spoke to every single chief executive and said 'Look, we've just made this announcement. Let me explain what it means and why we have done it.' We did exactly the same with our shareholders and fixed meetings with them throughout the week.

I thought we'd have much more resistance internally than we did, but the vast majority of staff said 'Good for you. We need leadership when times are tough; we want our top management to take tough decisions.' Business is about being strong-minded, telling it like it is, and that's exactly what we have done. Brian Pitman came to see me on the day of the announcement and was immensely supportive. He said 'You're doing exactly the right thing. It's going to be really unnerving, but in six months, people will see that you have done the best thing. You've done early and quickly what others may find very difficult to do in 1992.'

Family and friends said to me 'You must be feeling terrible about all this.' They're wrong. You feel terrible before you do it, but you feel an enormous sense of relief when it's all over. It's waiting for the decision to be made public that is difficult. Afterwards you have a very strange feeling almost of elation at having grasped the nettle, accepting all the difficulties that will follow, but knowing ultimately without any doubt that one has done the right thing. One journalist told me I seemed remarkably ebullient. I said that wasn't the right word at all, it was just that I feel the business has grown up as a result of this experience. I have. We all have.

We have been positive throughout: positive about our clients, about the staff that remain, our shareholders, our banking arrangements, our future. What we are not is falsely optimistic. After the Gulf War, people genuinely thought the economy would pick up, and that by the autumn of 1991 we would be through the recession. But the recovery has not happened, so you either say 'Well, it will be here next quarter', which is what a lot of businesses are doing, or you take action.

If the service industries are gloomy, they're reflecting the attitudes of their clients. It's a very depressing economic forecast of minimal, if not actually negative, growth for 1992 in some of the key markets of the world. There is not going to be a great lift-off.

It's not easy to look at the market-place and the financial information available and say 'How does this affect the way I run my company?' But that's what you have to do. It's not about what you read in the books or the magazines or the forecasts. They're all meaningless until you do something about it.

A recession makes you do all those things that you should have done earlier. It's very uncomfortable, very tough, but it makes you realise that you are a proper businessman. You're trying to do what is best for everybody, particularly the shareholders. If there's one little world of happiness, it's that having joined the Exchange Rate Mechanism, I don't think we will see these big economic swings again. If you can get your business through this recession in reasonable shape, you will be able to build well throughout the rest of the decade.

I never worried about people being too materialistic in the 1980s, because if you're not in business to make money, I'm not terribly sure why you're doing it. You're in business so that you make money, the company makes money, the shareholders make money, the staff makes money and the clients make money. If any one of those particular relationships doesn't work on that basis, then you shouldn't be in it at all. Everybody has got to be financially better off in business. Each constituent has got to feel that the relationship is making him richer.

Running a business in the 1990s may seem boring, compared to the 1980s. Then, life was full of fun. It's different now; that's not what this world is all about. The 1980s were all about enhancing earnings per share at the cost of every other consideration. That didn't just apply to us as a public company, it applied to all our clients. In a bull market, people want to get the highest possible share price so they can use their paper in order to buy other businesses and expand. The higher their price earnings (PE) ratio, the more they can pay for other companies without losing their own earnings per share enhancement. That's what drives the market up, and because of the accounting legislation in this country, you are able to develop the business with some fairly flexible areas for judgement over how you financially account for those acquisitions.

The 1980s actually finished in October 1987, when the Stock Market crashed. The difference in the 1990s is that while people are still looking for earnings per share improvement, they are looking at a slightly longer-term timetable. They are aware that there are more important issues than simply earnings per share. The environment, the community, culture, synergy . . . people are looking for something more than just short-term gratification.

The business environment has changed so much that there is a need for a different kind of manager. The manager that can build a business in a bull market is not necessarily the same person as the manager who can consolidate and develop it not just in a less bullish environment, but in a world in which there is a whole new set of priorities.

Mergers of big enterprises will still be the engine room of a lot of events in the City throughout the decade, because the market is increasingly demanding multinational services. Our business is moving into areas where we have never been before, and so are our clients. This brings totally new challenges: not just language problems, but culture problems, government problems. So the new manager has got to be international, and it's something that will come more naturally to the next generation.

The rest of Europe is better prepared for the Single Market than the British, probably because we're just an island. People under 30 regard Europe as a single unit, but those of us who are 20 years older still think in terms of the UK and the rest of the world. My generation never really travelled, but by the time my eldest daughter was seven she had already been to America, Africa and Japan. Young people think about the world in a non-sovereign way, and that is immensely healthy.

The manager of the 1990s has got to be very mobile, and extremely sensitive to different cultures. The way the Japanese do business, consensus style, is markedly different – not only in degree, but in kind – from the way the Americans, or indeed the British, do business, which is much more autocratic. So managers have to learn not only about the way in which business is done in these various countries, but the cultures they are dealing with. And the British are bad at that: we don't learn the languages and we don't understand the cultures.

The managers who were successful in the 1980s were highly impatient. They are the ones who went on building their businesses at an increasingly frenetic rate. These managers have got to be very cautious in the way they look at the various cultures that build their businesses. The successful manager of the 1990s will have learned a lot from the failures of the last decade. I think we have all realized that we lived in a strange world that may not come back for some years, if ever.

Shandwick set out to be the best and largest PR company in the world in order to meet the challenge of internationalization. I decided to take the company public because I couldn't build the business internationally if I didn't. Prior to going public in 1985, our fees were £2m, so we have grown very quickly. Whatever the future of this company, the real success of our clients and staff is ultimately going to be our position in Asia Pacific. I can find no argument that can deny the significance of Japan and China, or emergent countries like Thailand and Singapore. They are growing so fast that not to be there would be terrible. But the worst thing about operating exclusively in the UK would have been that our clients, who were looking for international expansion, would not have found it with us. They would have gone elsewhere.

One key to success must be to stay with what you know. I actually know this one industry extremely well. I understand it; I have a feel for it. I can look at the profit and loss account, I can look at the balance sheet, and I know what I can do with these things. If you asked me to run a sweet shop, or be a shoe manufacturer, I couldn't do it.

During the 1960s I worked for a bank in the City that invested in small firms. I remember one company, which was very successful at making boats, going into marinas, then into property, and the whole thing fell apart because they didn't stay with what they knew. It always frightened me. My colleagues may say I have been less adventurous and less brave than I should have been because I have always believed that you need to stay in what you know, even when you have problems. Every company in the world has problems in the middle of a recession. They are difficult, nagging problems, but they are a lot more difficult in companies which you don't understand.

A common mistake is believing what you read in the papers! There is so much hubris generated by the Press. You turn the page in the business section, see a picture of yourself, and this chap says your company is going like a train . . . it's terrific. And you believe it. You become part of a club, then when they write articles about the entrepreneurs of the 1980s, there are all these roll calls and you wonder why you're not listed. The media have a tremendous effect on us all; believing in your own PR is very bad news. You've got to keep your feet very firmly on the ground.

Perhaps the biggest mistake people make – including me! – is not keeping an eye on the cash. Because of the way you are able to account for non-cash profit, particularly in acquisitions, the collection of cash becomes too low a priority. Many of these companies that dropped off the edge of the cliff were making huge profits, but profits don't necessarily generate cash, and without cash your business gets weaker, not stronger.

But life is not only about profit or bankruptcy, it is working out how to be in control of your own destiny. And that is the big issue; that is the tough one. It's whether you are able to steer a course over a long period of time between being a courageous and brave leader, constantly risking financial security, and being so institutionalized that somebody says 'I can build that business faster and better.' This is the balance you are striving for all the time, and it is extremely difficult.

Meanwhile, you have to be prepared to give bankers and backers the bad news as much as the good news. A manager must be much more interested in what is going wrong than what is going right. You have to develop a realistic relationship with your bankers that will sustain you in both good times and bad. Everybody who works for you wants to bring you news that is going to make you cheerful, so you have to search out and face up to the implications of the bad news. I try to have a very relaxed atmosphere in my office, because I like people to feel that they are being treated as an equal. I gave up having a desk ten years ago, because I never liked the feeling of having something separating me from the people with whom I am talking. If you make people feel at home and at ease, then you can learn what they really want to talk to you about.

Having independent directors on the board is terribly important. A good non-executive director is somebody who tells you when you're wrong in such a way that you believe he is right! It's very tough, because most of the guys who run these businesses tend to be extremely confident, self-opinionated risk-takers. We excrete people who disagree with us. We squirt them out like pips from an orange, because we don't want the feeling that they are there to cause us problems. A really good non-executive director will say 'Hang on, wait a minute. I never say this sort of thing to you Peter, but let's just sit down and look at this quietly.'

Of course, I have made mistakes. The worst mistakes are choosing the wrong people. We've made some bad appointments, and it's been our fault. I haven't spent enough time worrying about whether I was choosing the right person for the right job. And I can think of circumstances where I've wanted somebody so much to be good that I have failed to accept their quite obvious shortcomings. If someone is willing to work for us and the relationship breaks down, you have to decide why it happened. In our case I think it's because we haven't paid enough attention to inducting them into the enterprise . . . .how we run ourselves, what we do, what we expect from them. We have never spent enough time making sure people understand what their job actually is, and how they're going to be appraised. This is a fault of many fast-growing companies, and I think it's a terrible mistake. When you're building a business very quickly, you tend not to pay too much attention to the organization you're creating behind you, because you're keen to get to the next step. But organizational structures are terribly important.

There will be some extremely interesting changes in the way that managers operate in the future. By the middle of the decade, more and more people will work from home, so the role of the manager is going to be very different. He's going to have a more distant relationship with his staff. And if people aren't coming to the office, then our headquarters could be anywhere. We certainly don't need to be in Grosvenor Street: we could be near Oxford . . . we could be in Hawaii. It wouldn't really make any difference; not even in terms of prestige. That is what happens when your business becomes increasingly international.

In one of our offices in America we have a scheme on test whereby 40 per cent of our staff are working from home, and it has worked out extremely well. It's wonderful for mothers. In a service company you are usually going to your clients' offices; they are not coming to see you. Who cares whether you get on your bike from 17b Snowdown Avenue or whether you do it from Grosvenor Street? Nobody minds at all, as long as they can contact you easily. The one aspect we have found difficult is quality control, because if that person is travelling to and from home, you don't have access to him. So you can't walk down the corridor and say 'Before you send out that contact report on your client meeting I want to have a look at it.' But the savings in cost have been astronomical; absolutely incredible.

It's a very interesting exercise altogether. You feel a little bit uneasy about it, because you're never quite sure when you speak to them whether they're in bed! But there's no real reason why we should feel badly about what is going on at the other end. After all, I never wear a jacket in the office, and I never wear shoes. But I was in a meeting recently and a chap said I looked very underdressed, so I said 'Shall I put a jacket on?' I mean, what difference am I making by wearing a sweater as opposed to a jacket? Is the quality of my advice any different? You might wonder whether it is polite of me to wear a sweater in a meeting, but that doesn't hold too much water with me. I think it's all about being prepared for the meeting, and being able to do your work properly.

There's nothing like being over-prepared. You should be better prepared than anybody else could possibly be for any event that takes place. This is absolutely essential, particularly in public relations.

Recently we had a case where a well-known brand of confectionery was injected with rat poison. Luckily for that particular client, we had in place a system so that if anybody tampered with their product we knew exactly what to do. We had a codename which put plans into action in every country where this company operated. Because of the different time zones, this codename immediately activated in each executive's home. They knew every single step to take in order to find out where in the world the problem was, get a briefing, provide it to all local managers, issue the relevant press releases and set up a press and customer incident room. All existing supplies of the product were dealt with, and the local managers knew what to say both to the customer and the media.

We had four dry-runs over a period of three years, and when it happened for real, the story was controlled so well that although the client is a household name, no damage was done to client, company or product reputation. It was a superb piece of PR because we didn't hide anything. Often, in our experience, a story becomes a story because people are less than frank about it. But if the media ring up and you are able to say 'Yes, our product was tampered with, and this is what we did about it: all the products are now withdrawn and back in the warehouse,' then the journalist will report it in a much more businesslike way. That's exactly what happened in this case, with the result that a story which could have been disastrous was dealt with in a very short period.

I like getting clients ready for the 'What if?' situations. We've done this with high-profile businessmen who are concerned about kidnapping, for example. We have worked with a number of security agencies to show what would happen in those circumstances. I like them to be prepared for anything. What if you're taken over? What if your factory burns down? What if you have a strike? What if your share price plummets? I find it a most rewarding part of communication, because you're really helping the management. You can't guess exactly what is going to happen, but you can have a fair try. And as long as you know what to do on the first day of the crisis, you can then adapt the rest of the plan to match the circumstances.

If I could have my time over again, I would have started my company earlier. I also would have read Part II at Cambridge in Politics and Law. And I would never have allowed myself to become so overawed by the abilities of others, even in my own family. I think sometimes children look at their siblings and say to themselves 'Why can't I be like that?' I wish I had been more certain of my touch earlier than I was.

One of the advantages to being 50 – though my wife would perhaps argue that there are very few – is that you go past the stage when you care what other people think of you. You might want to say 'Look, I think you're being grossly unfair in your evaluation of me', but you don't lie there any longer in a cold sweat. As long as I feel comfortable with the moral position I find myself in, I really don't worry. From what I understand, people think of me as being very hard, tough, numbers-orientated, ambitious and relatively callous. I'm not many of those things, but I am extremely determined. I'm determined to build a great company, and I'm determined to help young people get started. I like seeing people fulfil their potential, and very often they don't get the chance, but it doesn't take much time to help them do things they wouldn't otherwise do.

There's a wonderful scene in *The Godfather* which had a deep effect on me, in which a chap holds out his hand and asks for help. When the Godfather helps him, he says 'How can I repay you?' And the Godfather says 'The time will come.' I think that's absolutely right. When you are in a position to help somebody, do it, and expect nothing. There are a lot of people in my life who have done exactly that for me, and occasionally the time does come when you can actually repay something to them.

I'm terribly conscious of my weaknesses. I get bored extremely quickly, and that leads to a kind of flippancy. I serve on the National Health Service Policy Board, and there our meetings take three hours. I'd never had a three hour meeting before. I sit on the Arts Council, where the meetings often take five hours. I don't understand the dynamics of it; I'm very bad at dealing with things that involve a lot of attention, and I'm easily irritated. But I am learning a whole new way of doing things as a result.

I think my strengths have been, and continue to be, that I have a very clear vision of where I want to take this company, which I think is a jolly good thing for my board. They know exactly where they stand; exactly where the corporate thrust is. I am very determined, and the positive aspect of being easily bored is that you don't let the little things get in the way.

My job is like driving a motor car, preferably quite a fast motor car. If you concern yourself with what is happening just over the edge of the bonnet when you are driving a Ferrari Testarossa, you will drive into a lamppost. What you have to do is set your mind right down the road. The faster you're driving, the further down the road you look. You must be conscious of the turnings to the left or right, but there are other people around to study the side roads. Your fundamental drive has got to be down the road, and the people in your organization must be clear that this is what you are doing. You have to be able to answer the question 'Where are we going?' That is what management is essentially about. You've got to have very good teams to be able to do it, but the good managers are those with a very clear perception of where they are taking the company, and where they expect it to be in the years ahead.

## TIPS FOR SUCCESS

- Stick to your knitting. Staying with what you know is absolutely vital.

- Realize the importance of cash, and develop a realistic relationship with your bankers and backers.

- You must be in good physical and mental health, with a high level of energy.

- You need a happy family life. You've got to have a strong relationship at home, otherwise the strains and stresses of business life become too much.

- You must have a sense of humour. If this all becomes too deadly serious, you end up being incredibly boring. You've really got to have a good time, otherwise, why the hell are we all doing it?

# 7

# Sir Christopher Hogg

## *Chairman, Courtaulds*

*Sir Christopher Hogg is Chairman of Courtaulds. Born in 1936, he was educated at Trinity College, Oxford, after two years of National Service, and then took an MBA at Harvard University. He spent three years with Philip Hill, Higginson Erlangers - subsequently Hill Samuel — followed by two years with the Industrial Reorganization Corporation, before joining the Courtaulds Group in 1968. He became a Director in 1973, was appointed a Deputy Chairman in 1978, and Chief Executive the following year. On 1 January 1980 he succeeded Sir Arthur Knight as Chairman, and retired as Chief Executive in 1991.*

The second half of the 1980s was one of those frenzied periods of commercial activity which everybody thinks is unique. But they do come round from time to time, and in such periods people get over-confident. By and large, managers are quite short-sighted. They take credit for everything good, but when something goes wrong they blame external circumstances. And when things have gone well for five or six years, you begin to think you're pretty infallible.

I understand absolutely why under such circumstances managers over-expand and over-diversify. But there comes a day of reckoning, because recession is inevitable sooner or later. I remember when I was just starting out in general management at the beginning of the 1970s. The recession in 1973 was very severe in its impact, and yet, business school trained and smart as I thought I was, I simply didn't see it coming. Just didn't see it coming at all. The people at the very centre of Courtaulds would have seen it, but I didn't. I was very close to the trees, and my job was to prune the branches, the twigs and the leaves, and so on. Management is like that. Business is very much a day-to-day frontline activity, and it's very easy to get caught up in the current.

As far as both Courtaulds and Courtaulds Textiles are concerned, the recession of the early 1980s was far worse than the present one. It struck hardest on those companies who were most exchange-rate sensitive, particularly to the pound against the dollar. For them, it was absolute murder. I remember going to dinner parties in London and mixing with people from service industries, retailing and the Civil Service, and they really didn't understand what we were going through, because the pain of the recession was being borne in a big way by a relatively small handful of companies who were at the leading edge of exporting, and therefore of exchange rate sensitivity. Since then, we have made a great deal of changes. We learned a lot from that recession, so when the next one came along we were much better prepared, and the business was in a different shape.

By the time I became chief executive in 1979, Courtaulds had over-diversified and was performing poorly financially. It had far too many businesses which were simply not earning their keep, and very few which were striking successes. There was no obvious reason why we should survive into the 21st century. The first step was to cut out the businesses which were either making losses or were unlikely ever to earn an adequate return on capital employed. In a way, the recession made that easier, because the crisis was apparent to everybody, and therefore it was a matter of finding the will to be able to disentangle the real prospects for a whole range of businesses which had had insufficient management attention.

When a business becomes run down, it's very unclear how viable it can be made with decent management and a reasonable amount of time. You've got to touch your stomach and make a judgement. And you must remember that your instincts will always be to take out too little because it is so painful to do. On the textiles side, between 1980 and 1982 we took out at least a third of the turnover we had had in 1979. We closed down tens of factories, and we continued to take out capacity throughout the 1980s.

Then, when recession struck again, which it did for textiles back in 1987 as the dollar started weakening, businesses which we had done a hell of a lot to, and thought were fine, all of a sudden started to look shaky. But this time, we'd had the dress rehearsal, we'd seen the film before and we knew what to do. We were also much more realistic; we recognized that we might be in for a two- or three-year haul, though we didn't think it was going to last so long on the textiles side. So we battened down the hatches at a very early stage, cut businesses and costs, and this time round it was much better. The margins in textiles aren't very good in any event, because the international competition is so intense. And because you never know how long a recession is going to last, you can't just sit around worrying.

The part of textiles that has suffered most has been the spinning end. It's a massive business – £150m to £200m of sales – and we have about half the capacity in the UK. In 1986–87 we had 29 mills, and that year the business made about £15m of profits. Within 18 months it had plunged to making no money at all. It was partly because of the recession, but it was also the fact that international competition had intensified enormously because other governments subsidized their spinning industries, and the world was flooded with a glut of cheap yarn. Our business was virtually destroyed on the back of pricing which I think was unrealistic, but we've just cut very deep and very hard, and now we've taken out all but three or four mills. We couldn't have done it any earlier, because we'd have cut down perfectly good profit-making capacity.

The recession of the early 1980s had an enormously helpful effect on the making of the modern Courtaulds, though it didn't seem like it at the time. There are some things you can really only do when you confront a crisis, and there's no wind so ill that it blows nobody any good. You can turn almost every crisis to some kind of advantage, and a recession isn't an exception to that rule.

Recessions are not comfortable for management; far from it. But managers would get into some terrible habits if life went with them all the time. And when you've got companies which, by virtue of having brilliant products, or being in the right place at the right time, grow, as some of the computer manufacturers did, for years on end, then they get into all sorts of bad habits. And I know of no cure for those except a recession. You learn a lot of things in bad times.

Cash is a by-product of the quality of business decisions and the way you run your operations. If you run your business simply to make cash, then you may do a good job in the short term, as we did in the early 1980s, but you won't in the long term. For the long term, it's the business strategies that matter. Here one must avoid getting caught up in the euphoria and fashions of the moment in the good times and over-extending management or financing as a result. Fluctuations are a feature of economic cycles; they always have been. Whether you need to have such extreme fluctuations as we have seen three times in the last 20 years is a moot point. I would hope that the fluctuations will get a little less severe, but there will always be good times, and there will always be bad.

As a world citizen, I'm enormously enthusiastic about the expansion of trade globally. It must be in the interests of the future of the world, but I can see a long, hard road in getting there. Expansion of trade hugely intensifies the competition, and you've got to learn to live with that. For those of us in companies which on the whole enjoyed a fairly sheltered environment in the first decade or two after the Second World War, the adjustment to international competition has been very, very tough. And some sections of the economy are only now facing that adjustment; cries of pain are going up on all fronts, which is a feature of intensified competition rather than recession. It would be wrong to assume that big companies survive better. Companies survive because they do things for their customers which are distinctive, and which their customers want. There's no other reason. In many respects, size is a hindrance, not an advantage. Certainly in textiles, where it's very difficult to make two plus two equal more than four.

Management in the 1990s is going to be more competitive and more international than it was in the 1980s, and that's going to create intensifying demands. You're going to have to run your business to cope with the standards that are achieved internationally, and the best international standards are pretty formidable. In reaching them, every manager has the problem of dealing with the culture, the environment and the attitudes in his own home country, and they aren't always conducive to maximum efficiency. That can be very painful. I'm not just talking about caring for the environment or caring for the employees. You need to care for the environment, yes, because the world has rightly woken up to the fact that it can't go on behaving as it has, fairly recklessly, for a century or so. And caring for employees makes good sense, not from a paternalistic point of view, but because you absolutely have to get the best out of people in order to be able to compete internationally and effectively.

Any management now which is not really stepping back and trying to think in a detached way, preferably with external monitoring, advice and help, about the way in which it treats its customers and its people, is almost certainly failing to do a lot of things which they will regret in years to come. Take the simple business of surveying your customers and your employees. The best companies ceaselessly ask questions of the people who depend on them, as well as the people they serve. All the time they're asking themselves 'How do we look? How do we behave? What are we like? Are our standards high enough?'

It takes great courage and discipline for a management regularly to survey its workforce, and do the job properly – in other words, independently, through an external agency – and then respond to what comes up. Because if you don't respond, there's no point. However good they think they are, and however well the company is doing, managements invariably learn a lot which they find very painful, because it's all about their shortcomings and their failures. If it's difficult to face up to that, it's even more difficult to do something about it. But unless you're doing that kind of thing, which is not the norm in British industry, I don't think you'll make the improvements that are going to have to be made.

Business isn't difficult if you ask your customers what they want, and you listen to them. It's pretty clear what you have to do. Likewise, if you ask your employees what they think, and you listen to them, and if you look open-mindedly at best practice elsewhere, you'll get the right directions. It takes a great deal of courage and will, but that's what has got to be done. Of the companies who are doing it, those at the leading edge are discovering that there is a whole lot of debris being carried into the future; whether it's cultural attitudes or the educational system. All of these things have to be dealt with, which is a long-term problem. As Bernard Shaw said, if you want to change a man, start with his grandfather. That's why there's no short-term solution.

Successful managers run companies not only to be good at the time, but also to have the best chance of remaining good. They are people who can build habits of change and improvement into the mechanism of the companies they run. In the management job that I've had to do for the last ten years or so, I have had to worry a lot about the immediate present. In the early 1980s I worried a great deal about the cash, and I was very short-term focused. But once the crisis had passed, I increasingly focused five or ten years ahead. I was concerned about creating beneficial effects which would take place long after I had disappeared, and for which I wouldn't necessarily get any kind of credit or recognition. I think that's what professional management is about. Ed Jefferson, a previous chief executive of Dupont, once said 'In my time as a senior executive, I have benefited immeasurably from the wisdom and good decisions of the people who went before me.'

At some periods of commercial history, whole industries – and sometimes whole economies – behave like lemmings. The City made quite a fool of itself post-Big Bang, for instance. I guess it's because being chief executive, and forming strategies, is a lonely and miserable job, and it's all too easy to take short cuts. The shortest cut you take is very often the one which everybody else seems to be doing, which is why you do it.

So why does a firm like Cazenove not do what practically everybody else in sight was doing? That doesn't happen by accident: somebody up there is seeing things very coolly, very clearly and very bravely, because it takes real courage not to do what the herd is doing. It's a pretty rare quality, and there ain't too much of it about among chief executives. That's why people over-expanded and over-diversified: because it was the name of the game. The whole current was going that way, and it was very difficult to resist in Courtaulds, particularly as we had to change our portfolio to some extent. Constantly, all through the second half of the 1980s, one felt over-pressed to acquire and diversify. I'm not pretending that everything we did was good, though on the whole we struck a balance which has been constructive for Courtaulds. But it wasn't easy.

Few people react sufficiently clearly and robustly to a crisis. Most try to pretend it isn't quite as bad as it seems; they wait for a month before deciding what action to take. That's when a management hierarchy can be most valuable, because the next chap above has a much wider perspective. He can better judge the nature of the crisis, its likely severity and duration. But because the action to be taken will be less important in the context of his total patch, he's not going to be overwhelmed by it. He's going to focus much more on whether it's the right action.

I see this over and over again in textiles, where the view from the centre is such that you know you've got to be very tough. I admire enormously the managers who run the individual Courtaulds businesses. They do a terrific job, and I don't think it's a criticism to say that all the time they're trying to protect their people, to protect morale in the company, and so on. But it's the job of the centre to be tough.

Generally, the most common mistake managers make is not listening. Life in management is one in which somebody is always beating you around the head to do something, such as raise profits. And those kinds of objectives, particularly with a great organizational weight behind them, can be very overwhelming. You can forget that you must carry people with you, particularly as there are no short cuts to doing this properly. When you manage people, you really can only work through those people. You have to make sure they understand what it is you're trying to do, and enlist their help. But when you're really under pressure it's so difficult to remember that, and managers can be very abrupt in dealing with people.

The most common mistake with customers is forgetting that they are customers; forgetting that they are the people on whom your business depends. Sometimes you don't even show much interest in them, particularly if yours is a product which they've been buying for a good many years. You can fail to ask yourself some very obvious questions, like why are they buying it? What does it do for them? Is what I supply them really what they want? In my experience, it's a rare man who asks himself those questions in a sufficiently searching way. And it's a feature of hierarchy in a well-run company that when you've got two or three people in a management line, all of whom have a vested interest in seeing that the right answers are arrived at, you're more likely to find them.

It's very important that you don't fool yourself about what your competitors do, about the standards that are required. Most people do. You can never know enough when you're formulating a business strategy, but you can't wait until you do. In reality, you do it with great uncertainty; you do it by fits and starts. The business books pretend that formulating a business strategy is easy if everyone is rational, but that's all with the benefit of hindsight. As you peer into the fog off the prow of the ship, trying to see which course you should take, you really don't know the stuff which in business school case studies gets all set out. And that has become more difficult as competition has intensified.

If you rely on yourself alone, you'll probably get the wrong answers; you can't be Superman. But there are strategy consultants who can help. You can waste a lot of money with them, but there are some very good people whom all good businesses employ from time to time to check their own thinking and get an external viewpoint, based on their experience of other industries. So draw your net very widely; as widely as you feel you can.

I don't think that whether you go to business school or not should be a matter of fashion. But in the 1980s, particularly in the US, it became a sort of trade union card in some quarters – Wall Street, for instance. I don't see business schools at all like that. I see them as places which provide a training which can be immensely valuable in business. It has consistent, ongoing value. What may change is the world's perception of that value, but business schools are here to stay.

That's not to say that everything they do has beneficial effects; on the contrary, products of business schools very often come out over-rating techniques, while under-rating the importance of leading, managing and working with people.

They have a general management viewpoint as opposed to a specific functional viewpoint, and probably have too inflated an idea of what they can actually contribute to a business. Very often they don't have that essential passion about the product or the service they are supposed to be selling, which is what drives good companies. So they have fallen into disrepute for superficiality and over-cleverness, and rightly so. But not all business school graduates are like that, and it's not the fault of the training so much as the way in which it's applied.

Looking back over my career, the hardest right move to make was the Courtaulds demerger, because it seemed such an unnatural thing to do. Even though I thought rationally it was absolutely the right solution, and that was confirmed by my very supportive executive colleagues and by our outside advisers, when it actually came to doing it, reducing the size of one's management patch seemed so unnatural. I mean, that isn't what managers are all about. They're supposed to be increasing the size of the patch; not reducing it.

I was very pleased at having learnt the lessons of the last recession by the time this one came along. I'm very proud of the way Courtaulds Textiles has managed in the last few years, because it's a real testimony to what was done in the early 1980s. I'm also pleased about being able to hand over to a successor long before I needed to do so. I planned that handover four years ahead.

I could tell you a lot of things that one does wrong, too, but it's better not to dwell on those. On the whole, the mistakes I feel most keenly about are not so much ones of specific commission or omission. They are the mistakes caused by failure to recognize the things I couldn't do. In management, I suspect the most effective teams are those consisting of people who work together very well but bring different things to the party. You can't be a horse for all courses; the really big mistakes are made when you over-rely on yourself. I've tried to gather a group of people around me in Courtaulds who buttress my weaknesses and do things better than I do. On the whole, my colleagues would say I'm very inclined to analytical abstract thinking; I do it to such an extent that very often they don't know where I'm at.

I'm non-technical, and although I've done my level best to acquire an acquaintance with technology, I'm just not in the same patch as our research director, for instance. I need people who will act more spontaneously than I do. I need people who are more capable of going more vigorously down a particular track. I tend to see not blacks and whites but lots of shades of grey. Well, that's quite necessary when charting a strategy, and on the whole I think charting a strategy is probably what I'm best at. But when it comes to implementation, I can see a lot of things that I'm not very good at which other people do better.

I don't actually rate myself as a great people picker. I'm very guilty of wishful thinking. On the whole I'm an optimist, and I've paid on a number of occasions for that optimism quite dearly. I've made far too many mistakes about people; over-promoting them, over-trusting them, or just misjudging them, to feel at all complacent about picking people. I don't regret it, because it's a hell of a sight better to be an optimist than a pessimist about people, that's for sure. And I'm pleased with the balance of people who came to the surface in Courtaulds in the second half of the 1980s. The leadership now, both of Courtaulds and of Courtaulds Textiles, is something that I do give myself a pat on the back for from time to time, for having helped to form. And it is probably the thing from which I derive the greatest satisfaction.

I've come to terms with the way I am. The bits I don't like, I can get other people to do something about. I just concentrate on the things which I can do better than other people. If the rational and analytical image people have of me has helped to stop them playing politics, and encouraged them to think, then it has been an advantage. Whatever else people know about me, they know I expect them to think hard about what they are doing. I get impatient, for goodness sake, but under the stress and pressure of a top management job, anybody gets impatient. I certainly get angry sometimes, but provided people keep on trying, I will stay with them. They may be in the wrong job, so one has to move them to another one or something, but what I cannot stand is when people over-rate their own abilities and say 'To hell with you, I know best,' or if they're just lazy, or they stop trying. But if they stay with me, and they keep on trying, I will stay with them.

The first turning point in my career was going to Harvard Business School. Although it was planned, I couldn't possibly have anticipated the tremendous impact that it would have on me. Another turning point was deciding to stay in Courtaulds. In the 1980s, my frustrations were born of the circumstances with which we were trying to cope; earlier it was different. I might have left towards the end of the 1970s; there were plenty of good reasons for doing so then. I had some intense frustrations; I felt people had made mistakes which needn't have been made, and the temptation was just to say to hell with it, I'm going to leave.

But I simply made up my mind to stick with it, and I have no regrets about doing so. Courtaulds had put me on the board in 1973 when I was 37; I thought that represented a hell of an act of faith, and I didn't think I'd done much to justify it towards the end of the 1970s. And although the 1980s were very difficult, now we're through them, and Courtaulds is in an incomparably healthier state, I feel pleased to have been able to meet that challenge, and help to bring Courtaulds to where it is today.

The only thing I don't like about my role as chairman is that it's too remote. It absolutely is too remote. Most people, if they are honest, will say the best times of their business lives were when they were in real engagement with customers, or factory production, or whatever. When they were actually in charge of something that was small enough for them to be influential over every facet, so they could drive it forward. It's marvellously exciting.

I joined Courtaulds at quite a high level, on the board of the paint company. Although even that was pretty large, with £60m of sales around the world, I could feel engaged enough to derive a tremendous personal satisfaction. Actually, I didn't want to move on from the paint company and I resisted being taken out of it and put elsewhere. The higher you go in an organization, the more you get perks of one sort or another; you're paid more and so on. But it becomes more and more remote. It becomes more and more difficult to see what it is that you ought to be doing, and to get the kind of immediate satisfaction which is, I suspect, what drives most people.

I have a great wish to get back and be involved with something where I can actually be engaged with the nuts and bolts. But I've no idea when that's likely to be, because at the moment I'm trying to be part-time chairman of three publicly quoted companies, and that is quite a full-time role. I haven't been doing it properly in the last year or two, and I've been able to get away with it for a variety of reasons. But now it demands some serious attention, and I intend to give it that, so I'm going to have to live for a while with my desire to get hands on.

What I do like about my role is the intellectual challenge. I like the sense of wrestling with important and complex problems, and working with people of high orders of drive and ability. I find all that very satisfying. For an able and trained mind, the real enemy is boredom. And the great thing about business life is that if you go at it, there's no reason why you should be bored.

If I have to do something that I'm likely to find boring, but it's important, then I will also find something else to stop me from getting stale. In 1984 I took on a directorship at Reuters, which was the first thing I did outside Courtaulds. I was very uncertain about it at the time, but looking back, I realize that not only did it give me the knowledge of a very different industry, and experience of a company which was growing fantastically, but it also provided me with a good deal of intellectual stimulation. I now see it was a very helpful background accompaniment to the long years of slogging in Courtaulds, for which there was no substitute. I was certainly better in Courtaulds as a result of that experience, though whether there was a comparable contribution to Reuters is another question.

There really is an infinity of things you can do constructively if you're a good manager. Almost anything you pay serious attention to and do properly is going to have a beneficial effect on the business. But whatever you do, you have to know the detail, both in order to make good judgements and to motivate people. Taking a detailed interest is the nuts and bolts of managerial satisfaction, and it is what drives a company. But to do that is just plain damned hard work, it really is, because there's no substitute for doing your homework; talking to people all the time, reading the stuff that comes across your desk, and so on. It's part and parcel of being a manager. And I suspect that for most managers the energy they have to devote to this makes it difficult to achieve a balanced domestic life.

It's very difficult to combine a balanced family life with a flat-out business career. Very difficult. Supportive wives can be prodigiously helpful, there's no doubt about that. Can you succeed without them? Yes, you probably can. But it would just be that much harder. I've got less and less good at relaxing as time has gone on, because one of the troubles about running a large organization is that it tends to become all-absorbing. In a way, so it should. If it doesn't, then you're probably fooling yourself about what you contribute.

Everybody has frustrations with the company they work for, for one reason or another. There will always be times when you wonder if you were really put on this earth to deal with this particular range of problems and people. You wouldn't be human if it wasn't so. I have certainly had some considerable frustrations in Courtaulds, but it's a company which has attracted outstanding people over the years and I count myself fortunate to have known and worked with so many of them. There's something extraordinary and unique about the Courtaulds environment; it's a very special place.

## TIPS FOR SUCCESS

- Stay fit. You need every bit of that.

- Stay cheerful. If you're miserable as a manager, everybody else has a hard task in being cheerful. There's no point in false optimism, because sometimes it's more than one's morale can take, particularly on a Monday morning. But just try. Try and see the glass half full.

- Listen. And I really mean listen, particularly when you think you're good.

- Work hard. Very hard. It's not only a question of the number of hours, it's the speed at which you work, the concentration, and so on.

- If you stay fit, cheerful, listen and work hard, everything else falls into place. The world is full of people who can tell you what to do, if you'll only listen.

# 8

# Christopher Lewinton

*Chairman and Chief Executive, TI Group*

*Christopher Lewinton is Chairman and Chief Executive of TI Group, an international specialized engineering company with sales in the region of £1 billion. Born in 1932, he was President of Wilkinson Sword USA at the age of 28. In 1970 he returned to England and was appointed Chief Executive of the Wilkinson Sword Group. In 1978 the group was acquired by Allegheny International – a $3 billion US public company – and he became the London-based Chairman of International Operations. He joined TI Group as Chief Executive in 1986 to develop a new strategic direction for the company, and was appointed Chairman three years later. He is also a Non-Executive Director of Reed International.*

As far as the general economy is concerned, it's going to be some years before the word 'boom' is used again, for we are heading into a period of low growth rates. Nobody can buck a recession, but you can do better than most if you have a clear focus on the business you are in and the strategy you are following. You have to be global, and you have to continue to invest in innovation to develop new products, because that's always the way to cope with low growth. You must watch your cash, which means you shouldn't get yourself into a highly leveraged position with excessive debt. And you must ensure that your managers are of the highest quality, that they're properly motivated and rewarded. If you do all of these things, you can't do any more. But you must know your business: that probably is the single most important element.

The first thing you have to do is decide what you're good at. When I joined TI, they were in the appliance business, the bicycle business and the engineering business. Appliances and bicycles are fundamentally consumer products, but TI's core business was engineering; they didn't understand the consumer markets. So we essentially focused back on TI's core culture – the business they really understood – and expanded on that. Today we are a world-leading engineering company with approximately 45 per cent of our business in the US, 20 per cent in the UK – where we are based – 25 per cent in Europe and 10 per cent in the rest of the world.

Companies with widely-spread portfolios must be extraordinarily careful. If you're a financial holding company with a balanced portfolio of various businesses, that's different. But the experience of this recession will cause those of us actually managing businesses to focus increasingly on our strengths. We won't be seduced by all those lovely ideas around the fringe that look good during a boom but cannot be sustained in bust times because we don't really understand them.

Diversification, providing it's within an agreed strategy, is fine. But you've got to start with the strategy. Every company must have a clear focus, understanding what business it is in, and what its strategy is. Expansion overseas wasn't the problem; it was how you expanded overseas, and the prices you paid. Diversification wasn't the problem; it was whether you had a strategy. If you didn't have a core strategy, but you expanded overseas, and if you didn't pay the right prices, and didn't have international management, then yes, you got into problems. In particular you generated excessive debt, and when the world slows down and the cost of money is high that excessive debt hurts.

If a bank throws money at you and you're foolish enough to take it, you can't blame the bank and say 'Look what they've done to us'. You did it to yourself. Sure, the banks were partly to blame, but no one is wholly guilty, and no one is wholly innocent. There's a shared responsibility, but our prime job is to take care of ourselves. My job is to take care of TI. If a bank throws money at us, and we elect to take it, then we're equally guilty. The client gets the service he deserves, whether it's with a bank, a law firm or an advertising agency.

TI saw this recession coming earlier than many other organizations. We took the view that while no one can buck a recession, we would do better than most, and we have. The strategy we embarked on in 1986 was designed to cope with circumstances of this nature. We are working in the global market-place, therefore my first task was to identify where we could become world leaders in our core engineering businesses. If you're a brand leader in your field, you can be a price leader. And if you're a price leader, you can be at the forefront of technology in your product innovation, which allows you to continue to lead the market-place. If you do that, and if you keep your cost base down, you will do better than most, because you have all the weapons. It enables you to attract the best management, because people want to be with winners. That's what it's all about.

We don't make products that are nice to have: we make things you've got to have. If you don't have the seal on the submarine, the submarine sinks. If you don't have brake lining on the car, the car doesn't stop. Our products are critical to the function of the whole; they're non-discretionary, and we look for a high replacement content. For example, if you sell a mechanical seal, after a while, the bits wear out and have to be replaced. Clearly we have been affected by the recession, because everybody has, but we are always taking our costs down and making our plants more efficient. And we're affected less because, for example, we're brand leaders with one product in Germany and with another in Japan. So even though one market goes down, the other stays up. It's this combination of geographic and product balance that has enabled us to thrive.

The recovery from this global slow-down will be different this time, because so much has changed in the world. There will be a natural correcting mechanism for the excessive growth of the 1980s, but it will be exacerbated by what is going on in Germany, the United States and Japan.

The significant difference between this recession and previous ones is that in the past there has always been an engine in the world to drive us out. This time there isn't, because the three main players are consumed with their own problems. Germany is going to be consumed for some years to come with the effects of unification: its influence on the outside world will be limited because it is busy taking care of things at home. Meanwhile, in the United States, we're seeing the emergence of the America First programmes. The feeling is that they have allowed in the Japanese to steal their automobile industry, their troops have been in Europe at the US's expense and it's time to start taking care of America, so they're going to go inward too. Meanwhile, Japan has clearly been playing on a privileged playing field. It has been allowed to exploit others' markets without allowing its own to be exploited. But Japan has been operating on very significant levels of debt and inflated property levels, and that economy is also going to look inwards and slow down.

Consequently, we're facing a much longer period than most of us can ever remember of very slow growth, and in TI we're managing our businesses accordingly. I'm not a pessimist – I don't think we're

going to head south – but it's going to be a very long time before we
see the heady growth of the 1980s again. The only exception will be
the Pacific Rim countries, which are looking at growth rates of 5 per
cent. But the problem is they're not a very large part of the world's
trade, so their influence is relatively limited.

In the meantime, UK businessmen have had their confidence
eroded by four or five years of high inflation, high costs of money
and a strong pound. Though inflation is coming down, the real cost
of money is still two or three percentage points too high. Interest
rates need to come down to get momentum back into the system and
restore confidence, but sadly, we're constrained by the ERM bands
on the value of the pound. The integration of the European market
will have no significant effect on TI. We manufacture and market in
every European country already, and our businesses are run by local
nationals. Maybe there's some possibility of it creating more opportunities, but it will be a long time before we really have one market.

The companies which will best survive this recession are those
which can cope with very slow economic growth for some years to
come. Companies which can will be viewed as having a materially
different value in terms of share price and market capitalization from
those which can't. The companies which are highly leveraged, those
in commodity businesses, and those which are essentially domestic,
are the ones which will have trouble maintaining value. So the slow
growth environment will create a greater disparity of value between
various companies, and it will allow the better managed ones to
exploit new opportunities.

In retrospect I would like to have made some of our acquisitions
earlier, because then we would have had them under our control for
longer when we moved into the recession. I would like to have made
some of our investments earlier too, because we would have got
better prices. I also wish I'd given more time to management
development at an earlier stage, but we were busy doing other things.
Growing international managers is a long-term effort. The real
success is to have international managers who – before they are 40 –
have worked in two or three different cultures for several years. They
will have come back with an understanding of those different
cultures, so when they hire somebody to run the various businesses,
they know what they are doing. But international managers are few
and far between, because in the recession of the early 1980s
everybody cut back on their management development programmes.
It means you can't find the 30- or 40-year-old who has worked in

two cultures, so you have to grow your own. Unfortunately, we're growing them rather late.

If you're trying to build a global business, you mustn't be impatient. Give yourself time, because to build a culture that is global rather than domestic is a very tough thing to do. The prime advice I'd give is to recognize the difficulties. You have to place very high priority on training your top people to have a global attitude. The first step is to make sure that the chairman, in his heart, understands what it means to be global, has personal experience of being global, and wants to be global. Then he can construct a board around him that is global. It has to start from the top, because you can't go global bottom up.

In future, I think boards of directors will attach much more importance to the quality of management. Managers will be properly trained, led and motivated. People will become higher up on the agenda, because managers create products; it's not the other way round. I also think much more importance will be attached to strategy. If you understand the business you're in better than your competitor, you will do better than him. I couldn't run a garment business to save my life; you can't be all things to all people. Those who think they can invariably fail. But failure brings with it humility, and that will take people back to their core business.

Many industries are only just learning the importance of communication. Cynics will say it's perception that matters, not truth. But the argument is, over time, truth will out, therefore it does matter. Perception is critical, as is truth, but you've got to recognize the importance of both. Poor communication is probably the single greatest management mistake. You think somebody understands what you have in mind, when you haven't even told them what it is. It starts with not thinking clearly enough about yourself; what your own purpose is, what you're really trying to achieve. If you haven't thought about it, you can't articulate it. So the most common mistake is lack of focus on your own objectives, therefore lack of communication of those objectives, resulting in lack of follow-through on the detail. It comes down to laziness. Another management mistake is to be arrogant; to have insufficient humility, and to think you can do everything yourself. No one ever teaches you how to listen, but listening and fully understanding what people mean – as opposed to what they say – is critical.

Successful management is an art form, not a science. People who try to reduce it to a science do not succeed. One of the things I look for in potential managers is good health, otherwise they won't stand the stress and the load. For the same reason, you've got to have a good balance between your personal life and your business life. You've also got to have a sense of humour, otherwise you'll never cope with the unreasonable nature of life. You must be well trained, and you've got to have sufficient confidence to hire people who are better than you and want them to succeed. You've got to be generous in spirit, because if you are mean, you can't reward people properly and you will be jealous of their success. Their success should be your success, but it takes confidence to realize that. If you can do all these things, you will generate sustained growth. But nothing is more important than track record. Talk is cheap, but what have you actually done?

Our management style at TI is:

- high drive and energy;

- confidence – considered risks;

- understand how to make money;

- hungry – high achievable goals;

- loyalty – team players;

- add value;

- no surprises;

- internationalists.

Motivating people is very high up my agenda. If you employ somebody and he costs you £100,000 a year, his overheads cost a further £50,000. I ask all our people to ask themselves every day whether they add £150,000 worth of value. Let's say we make a 10 per cent margin on sales; I want them to consider whether they are worth £1.5m of sales. In other words, have they added more value than they are costing me? If they can think that way, an attitude creeps through the company of 'Have I covered my costs?' Because if I am employing you, and you're not covering your costs ... problems. This isn't a charity; let's move forward. It drives a culture into the business; it's that consciousness of the creation of wealth, which is what it's all about. I believe in mission statements; you cannot ask people to achieve objectives unless they know what those objectives are. And you can't give mixed signals; you've got to be very clear, because if you all work together for a common purpose, you win. The Army does it very well. The Japanese are very good at it and so are the Germans. All successful companies do it: they decide their focus, marshal their resources and go for it.

When you meet people who are lacking in confidence, in many cases it is because nobody has ever trusted them. Nobody has ever believed in them, nobody has ever told them they're good or ever really given them a chance. Instead, they've been constantly criticized. If you give them a chance, they may fail: you must be willing to allow managed failure. But if they actually get it right, confidence comes at a tremendous rate. If you work for somebody who is confident, the chances are you will be more confident. If you work for somebody who is a winner, the chances are you will be a winner. It's important to work in a winning environment, in a culture that has confidence.

Successful management is all about identifying, training and developing leaders, and it's a very tough thing to do. You can give people confidence, but it isn't quite the same. You can certainly train people to have better leadership qualities, and the Army does that extremely well. If I could afford the time to use the War Office Selection Board's system of interviewing I would, but I don't have that much time. The Army picks out leadership qualities very cleverly, but you can't make people what they're not. Some people are natural leaders, others aren't. You can make people better at what they're trying to do, but you can't cross that last little gap.

For some of the younger managers this recession will have been an invaluable experience, but if they are working for people who run for the foxholes, they have no chance. Ages and ages ago, I was told by a garden-tool salesman in Brooklyn that life is all about three choices. Imagine standing on an aircraft runway with a steamroller coming towards you. You can either say 'Stop', in which case the roller goes over the top of you (and you're never seen again), or you can look at it in terror and run for the hills (and you're never seen again). But the third choice is that you stand aside, and as the steamroller comes by, you go up to the driver and say 'Can I help you steer that a little bit?' And that is the ultimate management skill. So when you see a board or management team going in a particular direction, you don't say 'Stop', neither do you head for the hills. Instead, you say 'Can we discuss this a little bit more?'

There were two turning points in my life. The first was doing National Service in the Army, which was absolutely tremendous. I was a commissioned officer from 1953 to 1955, and in that time I gained ten years' worth of experience. It taught me about people management and attitudes, and to this day I'm a great believer in structure and discipline. I learned a lot from the Army and I owe it a great debt. The second turning point was emigrating to the United States in 1960. I only came back because in 1971 I was asked to run the Wilkinson Sword Group based in London. I've spent half of my working life in the United States, and I was planning to go back. So much for personal plans!

I've always had some very close friends from whom I seek advice, and I would encourage all young men to do this. There are three or four people in the world whom I regard as personal confidantes and for whom I have great respect. When I am faced with choices that are quite complex, I usually talk to them, along with my wife. They are the people who give me the primary influence, though I would say that my wife is way ahead of anybody else when it comes to giving me advice.

When you are chairman, you also need the frank, experienced advice which the best non-executive directors can give. Ours in TI have been first class. Sir John Cuckney, Michael Davies and Derek Edwards advised Ronny Utiger, then chairman, back in 1985 that the group needed to bring in a new chief executive to change the culture, and that is why I am in TI today. I believe in having 50 per cent executive directors and 50 per cent non-executives on the board, which is rather more non-executives than most UK organizations and more executives than most US organizations. Non-executive directors are hugely important to the future of a company, but they are vastly under-rated in this country and over the next decade that has got to change.

I've never understood why we pay management consultants several thousand pounds a day when we pay non-executive directors half that rate. The consultants are transaction driven; they have no liability whatsoever, and no long-term commitment to the company. Non-executive directors have legal liabilities and a long-term commitment, but we pay them half as much. It's a complete nonsense.

What we've got to do is realize their importance and pay them properly, which in my view is roughly double what most people pay them today. Non-executive directors are critical to the future of a company. It is non-executive directors who drive succession management. It is they who will choose my successor, not me. It is they who will influence me on the succession of the people who report to me, and it is they who bless my strategy and support the culture change. Non-executive directors keep me focused, and if they see me going off the rails, it is they who will do something about it.

The fundamental job of a chairman is three-fold: he sets the strategy, determines the culture and selects the key people. That has been my greatest contribution to TI. If I look at my track record, I would say my greatest strengths are that I think internationally, I act strategically, and I like choosing good people and helping them win. I like to see people succeed. I get immense pleasure from seeing them having happier lives by being part of the team. My biggest weakness is that I'm impatient; I have a short fuse, particularly when I'm tired. I get annoyed if people don't answer questions. I don't trust people who don't take notes; they think they can remember it all, which is absolute rubbish because no one can. And I don't like people who don't follow things through.

I've spent a lot of my life in the United States, and as a result we have a very open culture within TI. I communicate reasonably well, I'm very approachable and my door is always open. I'm international by choice, and I think the Anglo-American dimension of my background is an advantage. The experience I've had has been a real plus, because it gives me credibility. Life is all about trust and confidence, and if people are to trust you and have confidence in you, credibility is essential. Being seen as a winner enables people to follow you, support you and work with you. I'm very much a team player; I don't think one man can accomplish anything. The real trick is getting a team to believe in the common purpose, and driving them towards that goal.

What I like about my role is the constant sense of achievement. When you've worked all day and you are tired, it doesn't seem to matter as long as you have actually achieved something. I like winning, and I try to add a lot of value at TI. The people I work with are very bright, and that keeps me alive. This business allows me to work with people of different ages with a huge spread of interests, both internationally and domestically. It's colourful, and it's forever changing. I like change; I find it very exciting. It helps you to think creatively.

Having a balanced life is hugely important. My wife, Louise, is very much part of my life in the sense that she's part of my business life too. The fact that she understands my business life makes our personal life even better. She can be completely independent and say what she really thinks, and that's very important. Women have an insight, there's no question about it. They look at men differently, so you get an insight that you wouldn't get from a man.

In my spare time I like playing golf and tennis, and reading. I enjoy the sunshine and beaches . . . water, swimming and boats. We have four boys in their early 20s; when we can, we all go on vacations together, and I enjoy that immensely. For me it is fascinating to see them facing the changes that are going to take place in the world over the next few decades. . . . seeing how they're going to be part of it, and how they're going to shape themselves. I like giving them advice, although I think they question most of it, perhaps because I am over 30! But I enjoy being with the family; I like being away from work, and I like being at work. I get pleasure from both.

There are only two things I would change if I could. Firstly, I would like to have more free time, but I have the constraints of running a business, and life isn't perfect. Secondly, I find it very challenging managing the six-monthly financial reporting requirements in the UK and the quarterly requirements in the US against doing what is right for the long-term strategic interests of the business.

One Japanese manufacturer had eight years of negative cash flow before leading the market with disposable lighters: I wouldn't stay employed if I did that. Germany and Japan are driven by product quality and long-term world market share. We are driven by financial reporting requirements, which is an entirely different objective. The god we worship in the UK and the US is financial performance on a quarterly or six-monthly basis. I'm not complaining, but it's important to recognize the differences. I wouldn't live in Germany or Japan, whereas I am happy to live in the UK or US, and I choose to be here. But over the next ten or twenty years I think Germany and Japan will come a bit towards us, and we'll go a bit towards them until we find some middle way.

The future of the world will be influenced enormously by the recent media explosion. That is the underlying reason why the Berlin Wall came down. There are going to be enormous business opportunities over the next few decades as a result of this media explosion. The world has a billion 'haves' and four billion 'have nots'. With satellites in the sky beaming programmes everywhere, the four billion 'have nots' are going to know what is available in the rest of the world. People sitting in mud huts 1,000 miles up the Amazon with big receivers on the roof watching *Dallas* are going to want the things they see for themselves.

The four billion 'have nots' are going to want cars, they're going to want lavatories that flush, and so on. For basic manufacturing companies such as ours it's going to be a tremendous opportunity: every car sold is going to need brake lining, and every lavatory and sewage works put in will need seals. Despite the fact that we're going to have slow growth while the engines of the free world in the US, Japan and Germany get themselves sorted out, when they do, the opportunities are going to be absolutely boundless. Somehow the world banks and financial institutions have got to be clever enough to find a method of financing the 'have nots' while they get closer to the 'haves'. If they don't, there will be a war. But it won't be a military war – everybody now knows that is not the solution – it will be an economic war. That's why young managers have got to be international. Because if they don't think in global marketing terms, we won't get our share of the world market.

In the future I would like to see the industrial world, the academic world and government working much more closely with each other. In Germany and the United States, senior industrialists go into government and back to industry, into academia then back to industry again. This inter-movement between the various bodies produces much broader and better balanced people. I don't believe the current British Government understands industry. It's not just the Government's fault, industry is equally to blame. The Government is trying to do something about it, but we've got to do a lot more. Similarly, I don't think the educational world understands industry. I've been to a few universities to talk to them, and the ignorance is astounding. It's industry's fault, because we have failed to make clear to them what exciting opportunities we can offer their brightest graduates.

I also feel very strongly that we have got to elevate the social status of engineers. We're the only G7 nation that denigrates its engineers and treats them as second-class citizens, hence we don't attract the best brains. If you don't get the best brains into industry, you don't create the wealth. So those are the two things I would like to see happen: industry, government and academia getting closer together, with regular exchanges of personnel taking place, and a commitment from the Government to assist in the cultural objective of elevating the status of industry and people in engineering.

When you talk about the three most senior offices of State, the Secretary of State for Trade and Industry is not one of them, and it ought to be. Everyone says the Treasury will produce the next Prime

Minister. Why can't the Department of Trade and Industry be regarded as the natural proving ground for the next Prime Minister? The reason is that the perception in Government as a whole is that industry does not have the same importance as other facets of life.

If I could have my time over again there are one or two things I would do differently. I'm an engineer by training, but I've spent a large part of my life in marketing, so my two basic disciplines are engineering and marketing. In retrospect, I would like to have spent time in the financial community at an earlier stage of my life. I would also like to have learnt one or two languages; I would have chosen French and Spanish. But apart from that, I don't think I'd change very much.

## TIPS FOR SUCCESS

- You must have good health and a sense of humour.

- Try and work at something you enjoy, because the probability is you'll do it well. Over a long period of time, it's very difficult to work hard at something you don't enjoy.

- Make sure you're properly trained for the job you do, and if you're not, add the bits you haven't got. Understand how to listen, and follow through on details.

- You must work very hard. I don't know anybody who has been successful in the long-term who doesn't work very hard.

- Realise that you alone will accomplish nothing. The only way you'll win is by taking people with you in a team. People think that in my job I give orders, but if I have to give orders, I have failed. Instead, what you must do is influence and persuade people.

# 9

# Robert Louis-Dreyfus

## *Chief Executive, Saatchi & Saatchi*

*Robert Louis-Dreyfus is Chief Executive of Saatchi & Saatchi. He left France to take an MBA at Harvard University in 1973, then became Managing Director for Diversification at SA Louis-Dreyfus, where he stayed for seven years. In 1982 he joined IMS International as Chief Operating Officer, becoming Chief Executive in 1984. When the company was sold to Dun & Bradstreet he made a brief attempt at retirement, but was lured back to work by Saatchi & Saatchi in 1990.*

During the 1980s, Saatchi & Saatchi became the Number One in advertising. Everybody was saying 'Now you're Number One your rate of growth is not going to be as big, so what are you going to do for an encore?' The people who were running Saatchis at that time decided to diversify into businesses related to the service industry. But what they didn't realize was that those businesses weren't comparable to the advertising industry; they couldn't be managed the same way. And that was a big mistake.

Meanwhile, in the second half of the decade, the general mood was that stock prices could only go up. You could go to the Stock Market, buy a company, take on debt, then reduce it by doing a rights issue. But there's one caveat in this, which is that the Stock Market must continue to go up. And Saatchis got caught with a high level of debt at a time when its stock started to go down in value. Then, on top of it all, the recession came.

When I joined the company in January 1990, my first task was to cut out what we didn't know how to do and try to focus on what we did. It was pretty easy. We knew a few things: advertising, PR, direct marketing and media buying. All the rest, we didn't know. The problem was, the recession was already upon us. So we definitely didn't get the kind of money we paid for those companies, but it was still better to get rid of them because it reduced our debts. It also reduced the amount of time we had to spend on things we couldn't turn around. But then there was the unpleasant part, which was that we had too many people. In the good times, if you're slightly over-staffed, nobody notices. In the bad times, it's different. We had to make 2,000 redundancies out of a total workforce of 16,000.

You have to be bold during a recession, and I ought to have done the cost-cutting of people much more quickly. As it was, I did it over a two-year period. Why? Because I was new in the business, and people were telling me 'Don't worry, next week this client is going to start spending again.' Coming from another industry I had a tendency to believe people more than I should have done, because 99 per cent of the time it didn't happen. I was probably a bit gun shy at first, and that was a mistake, but I certainly learned from it. I also realized that in this industry, what makes people happy is winning new business from new clients, whereas what we ought to have concentrated on a bit more is trying to get new business from existing clients. It's much easier.

Throughout the 1980s, the banks were lending people money without checking anything. You'd have five bankers coming in every week asking to see you, and all they wanted was to offer you money. It's typical of the financial sector that now, even with a good project, you can't raise money. The banks have gone from lavish spending to saying 'No, we're not interested.'

When we renegotiated our bank debt, which was a long and difficult process, none of the guys who originally loaned us money were still involved in running our account. They'd been promoted. But that means no one has to take long-term responsibility. For the people who take their place, the best thing is to say 'Well, we won't lend any more money; we'll let this company go out of business.' They won't get the blame, because they didn't lend the money in the first place. There ought to be some kind of follow-through, and there isn't. Not that the banks were entirely to blame. It was a mixture of the banks and the Stock Market, because if you could do a rights issue to reduce your bank debt for twice the price your stock was valued at a year ago, it was not a bad idea.

The tendency in the 1980s was to make all these acquisitions until finally you finished up with 60 companies and you hadn't got a clue how they were working together. If you're expanding overseas, you can either start from scratch, or you can acquire companies that already exist, and because of the market at that time, it was easier to make a profit by buying existing companies. The problem is, how do you create a team spirit in every country? How do you create an identity? I can tell you: it does come, but it takes a long time.

For the rest of the 1990s, I think internal growth is going to be more important than external growth. It doesn't mean you won't open up in a new country, but the days of buying 60 companies in a year are over. In ten years' time, we'll have forgotten all the lessons, of course. Because, let's face it, it's much more boring running a company and having to be involved with the day-to-day details than making an acquisition. So when we've all recovered from this recession, and we've had a couple of years of taking care of details, there'll be a strong temptation to start looking around again. And it will take a very strong board of directors, especially if the guy has done a good job of consolidating, to say 'Don't do it, because really you ought to continue as you are.' It's a cycle.

If the hardest part of acquiring a company is making it work with your existing team, what are your chances of doing it if you're making 60 acquisitions a year? You'd need a miracle to merge them together. So do one big acquisition if you need it, but until it has been well integrated and is firing on all cylinders, don't go for another one. And pick a target in the field you know. Don't go for fields you don't know, because it takes a different kind of management. If Saatchis wants to go into manufacturing – which is not the case – they don't need me; they need someone like Sir Graham Day, because he understands that business and I don't.

I have my doubts about these managers who are as good at selling coffee as they are at running a hi-tech computer company. Diversify if you want, but make sure you have people who understand the business. Personally I don't believe in diversification. I believe it's better to strengthen your niches when you need to with exactly the same kind of company, and be sure the people you are buying understand your philosophy. Take the time to integrate it. If it takes six months, fine. If it takes a year, fine; just don't rush into acquiring the next one. And I have learned that it is better to spend much more on a successful company, because you can make a big improvement in profits, rather than try to bring back a company from minus infinity to zero. It takes much more work and it's usually a waste of time. You will never make a running horse from a duck.

This recession has given people more of an understanding of value. Perhaps, as we emerge from it, managers will re-organize their workforces. Maybe you don't need to have this huge team of creative people. You need the top guys – the brains – but maybe you can draw from a pool of good freelances in order to reduce your financial commitments. Advertising is a business in which people are insanely paid, and they have a much higher opinion of their worth than is the reality. Maybe it's a good thing people realize that; it's bringing them back down to earth. After all, we don't control the clients, even if we like to think we do. You might control a local client if you're friendly with him and do all the right things . . . but a multinational client? You don't control him. You can be fired tomorrow.

I don't think we were quick enough to realize that, when our international clients expand into Eastern European countries, for example, we have no choice but to follow them. If we don't, we're going to lose them. We were a bit slow in reacting to that; our message was that we would do one campaign globally. But I've learned that there are very few products for which one global campaign will be successful.

My view used to be that 1992 was a fraud; I thought it would take until the year 2000 before we had a truly common market. But that was before the liberation of the Eastern countries. I don't see how we can not try and integrate those people, but there is so much disparity. Now I suspect the Common Market will amount to nothing more than a kind of free trade.

I'm not worried about the prospect of increased competition arising from internationalization. For a start, I don't think anybody will try again to build a network like ours; it's too expensive. And the advertising industry in a lot of other countries is still under-represented; take France and Japan, for example. It's very difficult for the French to be international; they're too self-centred. As for the Japanese, they haven't expanded overseas with their clients. For some reason, when it comes to the service industry, the English seem to produce the best results. And as more and more clients become multinational, it can only help companies like ours. My view is, you will have the niche players, who have a specialist role, and you will have the big guys; the international networks. It will be the middle-sized agencies that have the problem, because the international clients will increasingly go with people like us, whereas the local ones will go to the smaller players.

I'm still very gloomy about this recession. I think probably the manufacturing industry is going to be the first to come out of it, especially in the US, and the service industries will be among the last. But I hope it will at least have forced people to think seriously about their industry. Sometimes, in our business, award-winning advertisements are not what the client needs, and we have a tendency to forget this. It doesn't mean that advertising has to be dull, but we have a tendency to impose our vision on the client, instead of trying to understand his strategy. That is something this recession has forced us to do, because when a client sees sales under pressure as a result of the downturn, he wants to be pretty sure that what we are doing is right.

My feeling – but there again, I'm a newcomer – is that we don't do enough strategic thinking together with our clients. I'm always impressed when they get us involved from day one. Take, for example, the launch of a new car. If they say they're going to launch a luxury model to compete with X, Y and Z, we can be with them every step of the process. We understand their strategy, therefore our commercial when the car is eventually launched is going to be very much in sync with what they are trying to achieve. But if they come to us at the last minute and say 'We're going to launch in Italy, so you'd better get a campaign together,' we have a tendency to react with a glitzy model and nice music. So it works both ways. We have to try and understand their strategy, and they have to want us to be part of it. They have to realize how important it is. But I think this is going to change, and clients are going to involve people like us from the beginning.

It's always easier to blame a recession than to blame yourself, but the service industry had been complacent for the last 20 years. We had very good profit margins, good growth, and nobody worried. But when you look now, every service company seems to be in trouble, or badly managed. It's partly because 99 per cent of service companies have been run by the top creative guy or the best account handler. But his only mark is that he's done great work; he's not a manager. And I think all the firms in the service industry are starting to realize that they have to disassociate the work process from the management. The products they give to their clients ought to be handled by great creatives and great account handlers, but the company needs to be run by professional managers.

The way I describe a successful manager doesn't mean I'm at all like this myself, but I think the greatest strength is having the ability to be good with people. In a service industry people are your only assets, so have an open mind, listen to them, handle them in the right way, but then, when you've made up your mind, don't waste time: act quickly. I have a tendency to be a bit too stubborn. It takes me a long time to make up my mind, but when I do, it's very hard for me to change it. If the facts prove you wrong, that can be a big weakness. Another weakness is that I'm not a good public speaker.

I don't like having to do it – probably because I'm lousy – and that's bad, especially in this kind of business.

But one of my strengths as a chief executive is patience. I have goals for the company, and I don't get distracted. I might look distracted at times, but I will be patiently working away to achieve those goals. I'm also very international. I was raised in France, I've worked in America, Brazil and Switzerland . . . I feel at home almost anywhere. So I have learned there are many different ways you can approach a problem and achieve a good result. The French are very different from the Americans, who are different from the English, who are different from the Italians, and so on. But I can work with all of them, and it's probably one of my greatest strengths.

I was lucky; I did part of my studying in the US. Going to Harvard gave me confidence, because I didn't have any experience of business before. I was more interested in an artistic career, and I knew if I went to business school I would never be a writer or a movie director. But in fact, I was a very bad writer; I didn't have the talent. And I realized I needed some kind of passport to a career. I'm sure there are plenty of other schools that offer the equivalent, but Harvard was a very good passport. It meant if I applied for a job I'd stand a fair chance of getting it. Whereas if I went for an interview and the guy asked what was on my CV, and all I could say was that I'd produced a couple of movies that didn't go very well, I'm not sure they would ever have hired me.

People say going to Harvard gives you good contacts. I have not especially seen it, but maybe it's because I wasn't assiduous enough to go to those reunions. What it does do is teach you how to work, if only because of peer pressure. It's very clever; you don't have an exam before the end of the first semester, so you have no idea how you compare with everyone else. You've read in the books – which are actually total bullshit – that you're the brightest and most hardworking people around, so until you understand the system it forces you to work really hard.

My greatest triumph was being accepted in the UK. My fear, being a non-Anglo Saxon with a reputation for being a bit harsh, was that I would be rejected. I don't know why I have that reputation, but then, I really don't care what image people have of me. I don't want to care; I think it's bad to be concerned about your image. I bet if you did a poll of businessmen who've been featured in front-page articles, most of them are failures within five years. I used to run a business much bigger than Saatchis and I never had my name in the newspapers, but as soon as I arrived in the UK as chief executive of Saatchis there was a deluge of reporters. I've noticed in this business that the first thing people look at in the morning is the Press clippings. I don't. If there's something important about Saatchis I'm sure I'll get a call, but if it's about me and how I am doing, it's a waste of time.

There's too much hype about the advertising industry, and there ought not to be. Getting involved in a company's strategy and marketing their product isn't superficial; it's real work. I have a love-hate relationship with the Press. You have to be in the papers, you have to be seen, but this part of the business I do not like.

Few people can be in the same company for 30 years without getting bored, though it's an admirable achievement if you can. I'm definitely not that kind of guy. My level of enthusiasm gets dulled after five or six years. The day I'm saying 'Jesus, why do I have to get up at 5am to spend a day with the guys in Italy?' it'll be time to go. If you don't want to make the effort of visiting these countries and listening to people, you're going to be a bad manager because you think you know it all. But you can't run a service business just by looking at the figures in London; you have to go and spend time in the Japanese office to see what their problems are, even if you think you understand them.

The greatest managers will probably say they planned their careers, and I admire that. I've never planned mine. When an opportunity comes along, sometimes you take it and it's a mistake, other times it's a source of great joy. At each stage of my career I've had some failures, but I've had successes too. Generally, the opportunities that come along have been good ones, and I have enjoyed them. But was I smart? No, I was lucky. Working for Saatchis is a case in itself. When I sold IMS, I decided never to work again. We had taken the company from a capitalization of £80m on the Stock Market and sold it for £1.8 billion six years later, which wasn't bad. But what I didn't realize is that when you retire at 40, all your friends are still working and it's extremely difficult to occupy yourself. In the first year, I travelled. I had travelled a lot before, but always on business, so I hadn't had a chance to explore.

I had never met the Saatchi brothers but they once tried to buy my company, and they rang from time to time, saying 'Why don't you do some work?' Finally I decided to start working again in

January 1990, but before I had a chance to look around they contacted me again. So I went to see them, and the next thing I knew I was chief executive of Saatchi & Saatchi. Did I plan it? No, it was luck.

I come from a family business, and Saatchi & Saatchi is basically two brothers. It sounds romantic, but it's nice to have played a small part in getting the company out of trouble. I take personal satisfaction from that. There are some quite extraordinary people in the company, and it's been very interesting for me. In my last business you had people who were well-rounded; a good bowler was also a good batsman and a good fielder. Whereas in this business you have someone who is a genius at bowling, but in fielding, forget it. It's a talented group of specialists, and it's interesting for me to try and make them become a bit more balanced.

When I finally leave, I will be very proud if, in addition to having put it back on track, I have created an organization which will be right for the year 2000. That is how I will judge whether I have done a good job. But it's very important to lead a balanced life. I don't think you can be happy if you're thinking about business all of the time. It's easy for me; I have a lot of outside interests. I spend every weekend in Switzerland, and I love nature, so I'm always skiing or walking in the mountains. During the week I play squash, and I watch a lot of movies. Of course, you've got to work hard, but if you're the kind of manager who is only interested in cash flows, then you'll have a miserable time when you retire.

## TIPS FOR SUCCESS

- Don't make the mistake of thinking your existing organization is the right one for the future. Companies should constantly reassess themselves in order to move with the times.

- Remember that in the service industry, people are your greatest assets. Your success as a manager will be determined by how you handle them.

- If you make an acquisition, stick to the field you know and make sure you take the time to integrate it into your existing organization before acquiring any more.

- Never believe you can walk on water; always remember the failures. Just because you've been successful doesn't mean it will continue.

- Keep a sense of humour; it gives you a fantastic perspective. Unfortunately, a lot of people can laugh at everyone else, but not at themselves.

# 10

# Geoffrey Maitland Smith

*Chairman, Sears*

*Geoffrey Maitland Smith is Chairman of Sears. Born in 1933, he attended University College School, London, and is a Fellow of the Institute of Chartered Accountants in England and Wales. In 1959 he became a Partner of Thornton Baker – now Grant Thornton – where he stayed until 1971, when he was appointed to the board of Sears. His non-executive directorships include Asprey, Midland Bank and Hammerson, and in the past he has been a Director of Courtaulds and Central Independent Television. In addition, he is Chairman of Council at University College School, London, and President of The Intercontinental Group of Department Stores. He was appointed Chairman of Sears in 1985.*

Consumption levels went roaring away in the 1980s. We really overdid it, so the swing of the pendulum took us back dramatically, and very quickly. As a result, it is likely to be tough for a long time. Unfortunately, I think the cycles of boom and recession will continue like that. It seems unlikely we will ever iron them out completely, although we ought to be able to avoid such violent swings, which no one wants and everyone regrets.

Encouraged by growing levels of consumer spending, the retailing industry developed a much too short-term view and went for what in retrospect was a quick buck. It did up shops to make them look glamorous, not realizing that three years later they'd have to be written off. Shops need to be designed to have more flexibility, so that, in an ideal world, you can change them around. Marks and Spencer is an excellent example: you have a basic shell, inside which is a shop, but you can go there tomorrow morning and notice distinct changes, when in fact what they've done is to move the merchandise around according to what is selling best.

Retail trading areas now need to be a bit more traditional to last long enough to afford the initial cost of fitting out. Shops need to present merchandise attractively and, at the same time, in such a way that the customer can select by touching and trying. Next to layout comes lighting, but above all comes the merchandise itself. You need to find a formula, then roll it out through the branches. But you've got to be prepared to improve it, alter it from time to time, and make sure that the basic structure is a long-lasting traditional one which doesn't need to be written off quickly. Where retailers went wrong was chasing after too many gimmicks all at once.

If I was trying to explain the problems of a recession, personally I'd say it's a period when your whole focus needs to be on distinguishing between solvency and liquidity. For a long time people thought they meant the same, but it is not so. If someone has a £100,000 house and no mortgage, he's solvent. But if he hasn't got any money in the bank to pay his electricity bill, he has no liquidity; he's broke. In business, of course, we have to worry about paying wages at the end of the month, and paying our suppliers. It's liquidity that matters, and that's what sorts out those who survive from those who don't.

The previous recessions were more predictable. This one crept up on us very quickly. It stemmed, in my opinion, from the budgets of Nigel Lawson. Taxes were reduced too quickly, without using the reductions to eliminate reliefs which were no longer morally sustainable, for example, mortgage interest relief. With escalating house values, owner-occupiers were fooled into believing they were richer than they were, with a consequent excess of personal borrowing and spending, and a reduction in levels of savings. We invented a new way of life, which was to feel rich and therefore think we could afford to spend money, even if we hadn't got it.

The Government took this recession very seriously, and instead of easing it out gently, took radical steps which have actually made the cure very fierce indeed. That is of course why recently we have been suffering, but what I find interesting is how it is working out.

Interest rates were extraordinarily high. The consumer paying his mortgage found his payments had gone up by 50 per cent, and it was a dramatic increase to find each month. Now, of course, it's getting better, but is he spending that extra money? Not at all, because he fears the possibility of being made redundant, and he's waiting for something to happen to restore his confidence. So savings ratios are high, which is another sign that consumers aren't spending. We can't even persuade customers to take goods on credit, which is good for society, but not for business.

The previous recessions were all about slimming industry down, and it meant that a large number of people, particularly what they call blue-collar workers, suffered redundancies. This time round it's been much more focused on middle-class and white-collar workers, who found that pillars of their local society, like accountants, architects and even lawyers, had been laid off. They couldn't believe it. But it actually happened – it is still happening – and that has affected their levels of confidence. In turn, the gloom is conveyed quickly and effectively to neighbours and friends, and the downward spiral of confidence spreads.

In certain areas, Sears has been adversely affected. In other areas, we haven't. The general body of customers is spread over quite a wide spectrum. For basic necessities, it's been business as usual. It's all about controlling costs and promoting our merchandise. Buying well: I'm a great believer in having what the public is looking for. I put that first. One of our special businesses that has done very well is Adam's Childrenswear, because childrenswear is a necessity. If you get the merchandise right – the colour, the co-ordination, the quality and the price – it attracts more business. And parents tend to put children first in a recession.

Freemans, our mail order business, has been very strong indeed, which supports my point that it's only a certain stratum of society which has been affected. The people who use mail order are usually sitting at home, perhaps watching television, then get on the phone to do the shopping. They're going to spend so much a week, whether it's £10 or £20, and that hasn't changed.

Selfridges has been adversely affected, much to do with the lower number of tourists. Our customers tend to be based in central London, and if they need something, they'll buy it. If they only want it, but don't need it, they won't. There's a big difference between the two. Sportswear has become a bit of a fashion; 25 per cent of the footwear sold in this country is now trainers. In America it's 40 per cent, but I don't think our percentage will increase to that extent. I think it will actually flatten out because trainers are very expensive for a basic need. Consumers want Reebok, Nike or Adidas because of the label; it's fantastic branding. But with trainers selling at £70 a pair – and some of them are £130 – people are hanging on to their money and making do.

So we have been affected, but then, Sears is very strong financially. It comes back to my liquidity point; suppliers are particularly keen to deal with you if you're strong financially. There's no hesitation. They don't say, 'We're sending our lorry in today, but we want cash on the nail.' We will pay on the due date, and they can rely on it. This helps us to buy at keen prices. We're also buying cheaper because of recessions elsewhere. In America, the weaker dollar has meant they haven't been in the Far East taking up large quantities of supplies, which puts pressure on us to pay more. So we're going to the Far East to buy our normal product ranges and finding that the factories are delighted to see us. They're offering us merchandise which in many cases is 10 to 15 per cent less than it was a year ago.

But it's been much more difficult to make a realistic profit, because we do need a certain level of turnover. And retailing has been more adversely affected by cost increases than any other industry. Retailing is a big industry – it employs more than 10 per cent of the workforce in this country – and we've had massive increases in rates. It's now called UBR – uniform business rate - and it's very high, because the valuation date was March 1988, which was the peak of the boom for retailers. So we're all suffering from that.

The Government recognized the problem to some extent and spread it over five years, but it's still very onerous. Meanwhile, there have been wage increases and so on. But we're noticing much more stability with our employees; their turnover is much reduced. Retailing, generally, is an industry with a very high turnover of employees in their first year, because the young person coming in doesn't realize how tough it is. You're on your feet all day, and it's quite a sweat. The natural wastage as they leave is saving us from making other people redundant; we simply don't recruit. The rest of the employees are staying with us; they're not leaving, and that's been helpful.

The main redundancies in our industry are in central overheads and distribution. Overall last year we were forced to make 3,000 redundancies out of a total workforce of 51,000, which is nearly 6 per cent. But there are minimum levels at which you can operate. If you get to the point where you really are so lean you've got one person manning a shop and three customers come in, they won't come back because they don't get served.

Within the Sears group we spend a lot of time working on customer care, because the people who really matter are the consumers. Without them, there isn't a business. Our jobs will have gone. And we're bringing back from her home the lady whose children are growing up, who is very much aware of what it is like to be served by a disinterested salesperson. Her life is a bit boring: she makes the breakfast, takes the kids to school and does the shopping. So why not have a part-time job? It could be two days a week, it could be four half-days, whatever. We're employing more and more of these wonderful people; they're so conscientious. They know what it's like to be served badly, and they do their best.

A conscientious employee can be almost a nuisance at times: 'Why can't you stock this size? It's what they're asking for.' You get some very good messages. Whereas the person who hasn't got his heart in it and doesn't care tends to say 'No, it's not in stock. I've no idea when it's coming in.' They forget that actually, if the roles were reversed, they would not expect to be spoken to like that. Or that they could devote a bit more time to the customer, instead of talking to their girlfriends on the phone. So the customer goes somewhere else.

There is always some element of risk when a new employee joins an organization. You cannot know for certain whether it is going to work out until you have tried it, but you've got to be prepared to make changes if it goes wrong. Making the mistake of excusing people who work for you – on whatever level – is, in my opinion, laziness. Either because one is literally lazy, or because one is nervous of confrontation, or thinks things are going to get better. If you have made a wrong decision, either with a person, or a business, then the best thing to do is to face the problem and sort it out, not just leave it there and hope for the best. There is always a temptation to hang on to things and hope they'll get better, but the first loss is the smallest loss, it really is.

In times of recession, the number of burglaries goes up, there's more pilferage in shops, more people get hit over the head, that sort of thing. But at the same time, when you're cutting costs, your security men are among the first to go. Internal audits . . . what do you want those for? Cut them out. And what have you done? You've actually increased the possibility of losing more. One school of thought – and it's one that I share – is that you should increase your spending on security in such times. It can have an adverse effect on the morale of staff if they are allowed to bend the rules. They like discipline; they work better in a strict environment where nobody cheats. They won't add 20p to their expenses because they could get caught. And they're proud to do it right. Not that our employees actually nick things, of course! But we don't always realize how important security is when times are hard.

There is always something about a recession that surprises one. In retrospect, there are actions I wish I'd taken earlier, but they're things no one could have anticipated. During this recession, we had the war in the Gulf, and on 2 August 1990 it was honestly just like someone throwing a light switch. Everything stopped. We had no tourists from that point on for some time. Aeroplanes were half full, then they were cancelled altogether. If we'd known the war was coming we could have anticipated the effects.

We have learned the need to have fast deliveries from suppliers. Shorter lead times are absolutely vital so you don't carry all the stock yourself. It will also influence companies to devote more time to what I call partnership sourcing. In other words, you will go to a factory, wherever it might be in the world, and say 'I normally spend with you a million pounds a year. Well, I'm going to promise to spend a million with you next year, but I can't tell you what I'm going to buy. It's going to be clothing; it might be tops, it might be bottoms, but I can't tell you the colour.' Then the supplier can budget. He can tailor his overheads accordingly. He knows the order's going to come through, but he won't know – except maybe in cycles of several weeks – what he's going to be asked to do. And those cycles are going to get shorter. Much shorter.

We've got to make suppliers hold more of the inventory for us so we don't have to carry it in stock. That would be very helpful; it means our overheads can be cut. They're trying to do the same thing, of course, but strangely enough, it's reviving the service industries. There's been a dramatic increase in distribution networks. Why should one have dozens of lorries on the road delivering whatever it may be when some other company can do it? If you haven't got the demand, and you don't need to deliver, then you haven't got the overhead. So we've moved away from a dependence on a number of things that we used to provide ourselves, and I think that trend will continue.

What you have to be so careful of is that you don't do a cut-price deal with a supplier, whether it's services or merchandise, who then goes broke on you. You've got to make sure he's strong and healthy, and stays that way. Suppliers are terribly important. There's always a temptation, when times are hard, to be tough on your supplier. There's nothing wrong with that – you've got to be tough – but you've got to be fair, too. If you're loyal to him, he'll be loyal to you, and you can have a reasonably happy partnership in both good times and bad. It usually means having fewer suppliers, but if you develop a good relationship, they know you won't accept rubbish. If the buttonhole doesn't match the button on the other side of the cuff, you'll send it back.

Consumers have become much more choosy through this recession. They're looking for quality, but they want value for money. They want to be able to rely on you; they've learnt that lesson too. 'Will he still be there if I have to take it back? What if I go to a shop tomorrow and see the same thing I bought yesterday and it's 10 per cent less? Can I get my 10 per cent back?' All these things have to be taken much more into account.

One of the excesses of booms is to allow individuals with particular personalities to have too much power. And all they do is complain about the fact that there are these blokes in grey hanging around – probably accountants, or something – telling them they can do this, and can't do that. These individuals are usually people with tremendous flair and ability, and they go on to build enormous businesses which, in my experience, can then decline or collapse. They collapse because of the inability to harness the forces within these special individuals with the necessary constraints, and the observation of reasonable rules.

That's another lesson to be learned from this recession. You can see it already in the City, where the guy's got to put up £100m for something. He's looking very carefully at the quality of the overall management at the top. He's less likely now to look at one man. He's less likely to say 'That bloke can't go wrong.' He might say 'That's a terrific team, led by a good bloke.' But he will have looked at the team.

Generally speaking, I think the banks have behaved fairly well. It's not in a bank's interest for a business to go down, but I don't think the general public realizes that. They think they are just standing by ready to pull the rug at the first signs of difficulties. What banks don't want is a loss, because it directly affects their profits. In some ways I think banks have been too lenient with customers, resulting in a number of companies surviving the recession despite being weak within their industry.

British banks operate in the most competitive market-place in the world, certainly as it affects corporate business. Also, more foreign banks operate here than anywhere else in the world by a factor of three, which, of course, redounds to the benefit of the balance of payments through the large invisibles surplus. In boom times this puts banks under a lot of pressure to compete in the drive for asset growth, which still constitutes the major earnings stream for a bank, but can lead to diminution of asset quality.

Banks have had particular problems worldwide for some time, and with losses arising through the recession, they need to improve their asset base. To some extent this has given rise to an unofficial credit squeeze, not one imposed by government. But the British banks' strong capital should place them in a healthy position to expand businesses for worthwhile propositions in the future. On the fringes there is quite a lot of venture capital available for promising enterprises. I suppose one could say that for the last ten years there have simply been too few good propositions chasing too much supply, and bankers, like any other businessmen, will have to be more selective in future. In the past they have chased after too much business in order to keep up with the competition. Even so, I wouldn't leave the blame at their door; it's companies that got it wrong, particularly in relation to an excessive appetite for acquisitions.

There's an old Jewish saying that you can buy yourself poor. The number of people who have done that! They think they've bought themselves another world, then go broke as a result of doing it. When a company finds itself in trouble, it often – sometimes without realizing – thinks it can get itself out of it by buying something. It certainly covers up the present problems. It also buys you time. Some of these acquisitions historically have been fatal. Only time will tell whether some of the more recent acquisitions by certain organizations will turn out to have been the right moves.

Sometimes companies think they can't go wrong. The newspapers say you're walking on water, and you believe it; you get hyped up. Equally, you can be over-criticized and treated unfairly by the Press. What really matters is having your feet on the ground; forecasting everything through cash flow so you can be quite sure that whatever you've committed yourself to you can pay for, even allowing for a downturn.

The biggest danger, of course, when times are good, is that you believe they're going to go on for ever. And one of the problems you face in a recession is that your managers – and I don't mean shop managers, I mean in industry – haven't always had experience of bad times. They were born into good times, and you promoted them in good times. They may have no experience, no idea at all, of how to operate with their backs to the wall. So educating managers to hold back and be careful is, I think, an important function. It's also one of the most difficult, because they just think of you as a constraint, holding them back. 'You don't understand; it's out there for me to make it ... let me go and do it.' It needs to be kept carefully in balance so as not to stifle initiative and enterprise.

The recession has helped educate the younger managers that it's not all fantastic, not all jam. It has certainly given them a different perspective and will produce a new breed of managers. We'll have a few years of much more common sense and understanding as a result of this experience. I have to say, however, that these are all very short-term lessons. There's another generation to follow who won't have experienced it themselves and so won't know what we're talking about, unless they've read this book! But so much depends on the quality of your managers. If they understand what you're trying to do, and have some experience of hard times, then they're not having to learn every day. There's something there that they recognize and can deal with naturally.

A successful manager is a good leader. He relates at all levels. He understands his job and can do it with a smile. He's flexible, not dogmatic ... open-minded is the word, I suppose. And he keeps himself up to date. The managers emerging throughout the rest of the decade will be better trained. They'll be professionally trained, and hopefully will have more basic skills. Of course, one of the dangers of over-professionalizing anything is you don't always get people with instinct and flair, and in retailing that's absolutely essential. But they'll be better educated, they'll have this experience, and they might even know what it's like to be out of work. It will tend to make them a little cautious, a little tougher, and less likely to have the excesses. Then the next generation will reverse it all!

The fact that common sense has re-emerged is one of the benefits of this recession. People have had some very rude awakenings, but I suppose if I had a criticism of the way it's been handled, it's easy to say, but I'd have done it differently. I would have said 'We have a serious problem, we've got ourselves into difficulty, and we've got to manage ourselves out of it.' But not brutally; not in such a harsh way. I'd have said 'What we'd like to do is perhaps take five years, three if we can, and this is what we're proposing ...' Though inevitably that kind of policy needs some form of controls, which, of course, the Government was against. It's a question of balance, but I would have tended to take a more gentle pace in order to avoid the levels of unemployment and business collapses that we are bound to see continuing this year. [1992]

Consumer spending may come back a bit, but there will be people who've lost their jobs, some have lost their homes and have had to take their children away from school, all sorts of things which are very painful. After previous recessions, I recall a period of a year or two when many businesses found it very difficult to cope. Just when you think you've got to the end and things are looking up, that's when you can get into difficulty. The effects of a recession usually continue for quite a while after it has ended.

In my opinion, there shouldn't be any dramatic increases in house prices for a while yet, although an upward swing can be caused by a shortage of houses which flows from a sharply reduced building programme. While the present difficulties have dampened our enthusiasm to buy a new house, I am confident that this is only short term, and that as a nation we will continue to want to be owner-occupiers. The current economic problems should see us with a much more stable housing market so far as prices are concerned for some time to come. This will be good for society and the economy.

There will be more independent businesses emerging as a result of this recession. Over the last 20 years the multiple retailers have been mopping up the independents; they've been disappearing. The chap who opened his little shop in the village found that his property, for which he paid £20,000, was now worth £200,000. He couldn't believe his luck; he sold his shop to a big multiple and retired. But I think all these trends are in the process of reversing, as the multiples have in many cases started to shed the number of shops they occupy, making them available to newcomers at realistic rents.

In future, retailers formulating corporate strategies will have to take into account a much higher cost base than they have ever experienced before. They've got to tailor their businesses to a more modest sales growth. They can't look for 15 per cent a year; they'll probably have to settle – if they're lucky – for 5 per cent on top of inflation. And they'll have to manage themselves out of the cost trap they're in. Rents will, as a result, start to come down. The property industry as a whole is notoriously slow in adjusting to these things, but leases will tend to get shorter. You won't have to take a 25-year lease; it'll be more like five or ten. And there'll be more turnover rents, so that a landlord participates more in your business.

The concept of the Single European Market is an excellent one, and I am looking forward to the continued move towards high common standards and freedom of movement for capital, goods, services and people. I see many opportunities for the multiple retailer that can take our skills of distribution and buying into countries where so many commodities are sold by independents. I also think it is important that these countries move towards a levelling out of the tax systems – and rates of tax – which will lessen the considerable complications that we have to cope with today. For example, if we've got a mail order business here and we are trying to ship goods to France, we have to pay their rates of tax on the sales. In other words, a destination tax. In time, we should be all on the same sales taxes, and then, of course, it will be much easier and more competitive. I see no disadvantage to the Single Market for us. We've got more than 400 shops on the Continent now and I expect that to develop much further in the future.

Branding has become increasingly important. There are certain names that you and I know well because we see them every day, but they're just as well known in Tokyo or New York. It might be Dunhill, it might be Burberry, but if the consumer has heard of it, he will trust it. Many big businesses today have been built on that, and I like to think the same applies with some of our brands.

The first lesson to learn if you're going to operate internationally is to protect your name. You must be sure you can register what you're doing. And you can't just register it; you've got to actually use it, or you may not get any title to it at all. Secondly, you've got to employ people in those other countries whom you can totally trust. People who have the skills to manage the business forward and develop it. Either that, or you must buy something. My personal preference is to buy, but don't buy anything small. If you do that, it can take five years to develop it to a reasonable size, and then you'll be five years older. It's far better to search out a decent base and pay well for it, because then you buy the culture, and they'll tell you if you're doing something idiotic. You certainly can't buy merchandise from here; it's out of the question. Nearly all of our buying on the Continent is done from there, because nearly all of it is for the local customer. There are some exceptions, if you're buying branded products, but it's a very important consideration.

I suppose, as an individual, I like 'The deal' very much. I like the acquisition or the sale of something. If you are able to pick the bottom or the top of the market – and it's not always judgement, it's often luck as well – then it's particularly satisfying. Let's say you have a business as part of your group which really doesn't belong. You carefully go into the market to see if you can find a customer for it, and you get a wonderful price. Looking back, it gives you quite a kick if you can see that you sold it very well; you didn't give it away. But feelings of success are usually only momentary. They don't last long because you're on to something else.

In difficult times, it is natural to start looking very carefully at your portfolio to see what does fit and what doesn't. I get tremendous personal satisfaction from the management buy-outs we've done as we reshaped the group. Particularly when the management is still intact, working hard and successfully going on to great things. I love that. And their employees become more secure than they would have been with us.

I think it is essential for a company to have an image that is known and understood by the people you're dealing with. But, on the other hand, it worries me if an individual is too concerned about his image; whether he was in the newspaper this morning, and how he came across. He's probably spending far too much time worrying about that instead of worrying about the business, so I try to discourage it amongst people in the group. We used to have a managing director in one of our businesses whom I found very amusing. Any time a cameraman came he used to go to the front to make sure he was very much in the picture. It annoyed me to start with, but then I found it funny; I knew he'd hang himself in the end. I'd much rather see the chap go to the back and get on with the job. It's far more important. The personality cult is not in my line at all.

Mutual trust is terribly important; I don't know how you can work without it. What I don't like is criticism without understanding. It usually comes from people who don't actually know what you're doing, haven't tried it themselves and haven't got the experience. But they none the less sit there and pick holes in your strategy. I don't mind criticism at all if it's fair, and well-directed. If the person's trying to actually teach us something, wonderful.

The turning point in my career was probably when I was approached by Charles Clore and asked to come and help run Sears. Until then I was an accountant, doing flotations, mergers and acquisitions in the City. I never looked back after joining Sears; I've loved it ever since, and I've never had any thoughts of doing anything else. I have other directorships which give me different windows on the world, and I think that's very useful. You pick up new information, you learn how better to run your own business, and in return you contribute what you can from the benefit of your own experience. I would certainly encourage people to take on an outside directorship, providing they have the time. But you've got to be fairly high up the ladder before you do that, otherwise you can get distracted.

Non-executive directors, preferably called independent directors, have made a very good contribution to Sears. It is not so many years ago that we regarded the whole idea with apprehension, but today their input to our decision making and their independent powers of observation help us considerably. I am very lucky; we have four superb non-executive directors who really do contribute because they want to, because they are interested. They bring a fresh approach and ask 'Why?' We discuss all major issues at board level to get confirmation that we are not doing anything we might regret. They invariably have points of view that add to the sum of our knowledge from within the business, and they may know something we don't at that particular moment.

I love the variety in my role, working closely with our chief executive, with the complexity of his responsibilities in running a group of this size. I actually find work stimulating, but I'm aware of the dangers of being all-consumed by business. I've had more than one marriage, and I think my past domestic problems actually stimulated me to achieve more than I otherwise would have done. Not just because I had more time, but because I had to be successful somewhere. These days, I try and strike a better balance, and wherever possible I include my wife in what I am doing.

In my spare time, I go shopping. I don't actually buy things; I just walk around. I have a keen interest in being up to date with what the businesses are doing, and there's no better way than visiting and looking, so I enjoy that. It doesn't mean I'm a workaholic; I don't think I am. At home I tend to potter. I have a workshop. My wife wonders what I am doing out there all that time, when I haven't done anything except make a lid for a box or something, but anyway, I've enjoyed it, and it forces me to create spare time in which to think. I also like clay pigeon shooting. It's something quite new to me – I only caught on to it a couple of years ago – but most weekends I go clay pigeon shooting for an hour or two and enjoy it. And opera . . . I go as often as I can. I find it a wonderful way to entertain and relax at the same time.

## TIPS FOR SUCCESS

- I'd put honesty fairly high on the list. People must know that you're honest and can be relied upon.

- Be punctilious in an operational sense. Never be slapdash.

- You need a lot of energy and determination. You must never be lazy; you can't say 'I don't feel like going in today.'

- Good health is important, because if you give yourself an ulcer, you may not be able to stay on your rung of the ladder, never mind go any further.

- You need a sense of wanting to achieve; wanting to win. Ambition.

# 11

# Sir Colin Marshall

*Deputy Chairman and Chief Executive, British Airways*

*Sir Colin Marshall is Deputy Chairman and Chief Executive of British Airways. He began his career with the Orient Steam Navigation Company in 1951, and seven years later joined the Hertz Corporation in Chicago. After a term as General Manager Mexico, then Assistant to the President in New York, he became General Manager UK, Netherlands and Belgium. In 1964 he joined Avis Inc, where he was appointed President in 1975 and Chief Executive Officer the following year. After the company was taken over in 1979 he became Executive Vice President of Norton Simon Inc and Co-Chairman of Avis. Sir Colin was appointed Chief Executive of British Airways in 1983 and Deputy Chairman in 1989. In addition, he is on the board of various companies including Midland Bank, Grand Metropolitan and IBM UK.*

I don't think in the 1990s we will see a repeat of the greed that we saw in the 1980s. I have no doubt that it will return at some point in the future, but we have certainly witnessed something which prob-ably will not return this century. That clearly has to be very beneficial for the world's economies, and for the business sector as a whole.

In the financial services sector during the 1980s there was a headlong dash by just about everybody to try to keep pace with what others were doing, or to try to outdo them. We had gone through many years of growth in the economy from 1983, and it was happening all over most of the world. A lot of people came into the financial service business in that time with no experience of what had happened in the previous recession, and they just got carried away in the tidal wave.

Another factor is that throughout the 1980s we saw deregulation come into the whole financial services sector almost on a global basis. That encouraged more and more competition, and the terms for borrowing got easier and easier. There was just this wholesale willingness to put out money without having the adequate security to stand behind it. And people believed we were just going to go on and on seeing a growing economy.

It's very easy to be critical of the banks and say 'Well, they shouldn't have lent all that money,' but it was going on all over the world. And I guess the banks in the UK got very concerned that they were losing out on the world markets. The American banks felt the same, as did the Japanese, and so on.

This time the recession ran very much in parallel with that in the United States. Normally one tends to follow the other, but this time they both came together and were quite severe; that is an experience I don't recall encountering in previous recessions. From our standpoint, not only the US and the UK came together, but also Canada, Australia and New Zealand. They are all important markets as far as we're concerned, so we really were hit quite badly. But it was the Gulf War that hurt us the most.

Until war broke out in the middle of January 1991, we were actually running above the previous year in terms of traffic, despite the recessions in all those countries. But when the war started, our business was down by 33 per cent in the space of two weeks. When it finished after six weeks we saw a partial recovery. But it was really quite a slow recovery, and even by September our business was running at below the levels of the previous year. I happen to think that if we hadn't had the Gulf War, which discouraged a lot of people from travelling – and because of that experience they got adjusted to not travelling – our traffic would probably have been marginally above that of 1990.

Within a couple of weeks of the war starting we embarked on a major cost-cutting exercise, and we had to take some pretty dramatic steps. Fortunately we had embarked on a cost-cutting exercise about a year before the war came, so we were already getting some benefits from it. We had recognized that recession was looming ahead, and that there was a need to adjust our whole cost base. We had learned the lessons from the previous recession; we anticipated that the growth in business was going to fall away. But we didn't expect to go into a negative growth position, as we then experienced.

So during the Gulf War we redoubled our efforts, seeking ways and means of reducing costs. We decided we had to reduce our workforce of 53,000 by 4,600. We then looked at putting a further 2,000 employees on a stand-down basis, whereby they would be on half-pay and subject to recall at relatively short notice. In fact, we never went as far as 2,000, but we got almost to 1,000 on the stand-down programme.

Meanwhile, we looked at other ways of conserving and developing cash in order to better secure our balance sheet, such as the sale of surplus assets . . . not that we had many of those anyway. But over the ensuing weeks and months we developed a detailed programme of departments or functions in the company which we believed we could either move outside altogether by selling or sub-contracting them to other companies, or by looking for joint ventures. We were considering any approach we could take which would reduce our own commitments in BA.

We're still working our way through that programme, but the most significant success we've had so far is the sale of our engine overhaul operation in South Wales. We've done very well on that, and we believe the new owners will be able to put more money into developing that business than we could ever have afforded to put in ourselves. So what we've been doing is really looking for ways and means of shoring up to be able to sustain and grow our principle business, which is the airline business itself. But had we not had the Gulf War, we would not have seen our business impacted to the extent that it still is. Given the suddenness of it, I don't think anybody could have anticipated that situation at all. But without it, I believe we were acting quite expeditiously; events just overtook us.

What this recession has done is to strengthen the convictions we already held. It is very unwise to be anything other than pessimistic when one is faced with the beginning of a recession. One has got to take drastic action very quickly, because it always takes time to put these things into place, and one therefore has the time lapse between taking the decision and actually getting a reduction in costs. So when you recognize that these things are going to happen, you've just got to move as fast as you possibly can. The only advice one can give is to make sure you don't forget the experience that you have gone through. Try and pay attention to the issues which brought about the problems you will have experienced. Certainly the most important advice without doubt in any business is to watch your cash position.

It would be nice to think we've all learned by our experiences of this recession, but I suspect we will have a repeat of it in several years, by which time a lot more people will have entered the business sector who will not carry with them the bruises. And though each time it happens we learn a little bit more, we also forget it as all the good times envelop us in the years ahead. One always has to try and find good aspects to almost anything that happens, and I have no doubt this recession has been beneficial in the sense that it has brought people to a very abrupt realization that good times don't go on for ever unless they are very, very carefully controlled. And even when they are very carefully controlled, they don't necessarily go on anyway.

The fact now is that we are more and more into a global economy, as opposed to our own individual national economies. What goes on in another major country around the world can, and in fact, does, have an impact on our own economy and growth. Obviously ours is a very international business, and the increasing levels of deregulation taking place all around the world are extremely important in terms of how we develop strategies for the future. Smaller companies really have got to look for the niches in the market in order to survive. By concentrating on those niches they can be successful, instead of being overwhelmed by the global giants that will inevitably be created in the years ahead.

The Single Market is going to be very important indeed. It would be extremely bad news for this country without it. There are all sorts of pros and cons, but in the overall analysis I do believe the UK would be in bad shape if we were independent in Europe. We have, to a very large extent, extinguished our close relations with the Commonwealth, and we certainly in my view cannot survive as a significant trading nation in the future without being a leading member of this Single Market in Europe. I'm quite sure we would not attract the same degree of foreign investment, and I think the decisions taken by the Government to allow the Japanese to come in in the way they did were probably very sound ones. My only regret is that we haven't really achieved equal access, or anything close to equal access, into the Japanese market. But these things only change provided you've got the *quid pro quo* to offer, and the other party – particularly when you're talking about a government – feels they can get something back in return of an equivalent value.

There are, of course, disadvantages to the Single Market too. It clearly over time is going to lead to a degree of loss of sovereignty, and I guess a lot of people will regret that. On the other hand, I do think that the advantages clearly outweigh the disadvantages. There will be more competition for British Airways, but it also affords us the opportunity to be much more competitive within Europe. Right now, we are having to compete with some real giant airlines in the

United States, and they are pressing very hard to grab every position they possibly can in Europe before 1993, when they fear that the Single Market will prevent them from getting any more territory. I don't happen to believe that that will be the case, but nevertheless they're moving as hard as they can.

From our standpoint, and from the standpoint of the European airlines, I believe that our best prospect of being able to stand up and compete with the size and power of these US airlines is by being in the Single Market. We will have the ability to expand within Europe and have more bases. That means perhaps eventually combinations of European airlines being formed on a cross-border basis, but it is inevitably the only way we are going to be able to sustain a major presence in this future global market.

Once the world's economies have turned round and we are back into real growth, we will see a recovery, a resurgence, of mergers and acquisitions. It won't be as hectic as in the second half of the 1980s; we probably will not see the same rapid actions and developments, but nevertheless there will be a resurgence. So I don't think it's going to be a stolid effort in the 1990s; I think the rest of the decade is going to be a pretty exciting period. We are clearly going to see much greater benefits deriving from technology, from the faster, more efficient communications links available, and therefore the availability of lots more information. More and more people will be able to work from home, but that certainly isn't going to help the chief executives carry out their business.

I don't think I particularly subscribe to the viewpoint that we will see a new breed of managers emerging. A successful manager will always be one who delivers a good return to his company's stakeholders, and when I say stakeholders I take in the shareholders, the employees, the customers and the suppliers. It really covers the whole gamut, whether the company is publicly quoted or privately owned. If you are in effect satisfying all your stakeholders, then you have to be running a successful business. You have to be earning a reasonable level of profit, and you have to be a good manager of your employees.

The most common mistake managers make with employees is poor communications. Not being willing to listen to what your employees have to say, and not being clear in what you say to them. I think that is the root of many problems. And the most common mistake with customers is frankly a failure to recognize what they really want, thereby imposing on them what you think they want. That's very pertinent to the service sector, perhaps a bit more so than the manufacturing sector.

I suppose I started moving in the senior management direction very early on, going back to the time when I moved from being a trainee manager in the Hertz Corporation in Chicago in 1958 to being a general manager and taking over what at that time was only a fledgling company in Mexico. It was my first break on the management ladder. I'd spent six months training in Chicago and six months in Toronto, when they called one day and said they wanted me to take over as general manager Mexico. They wanted me there within 48 hours, so I was there within 48 hours. That was probably the first significant turning point.

The next one was ITT's acquisition of Avis in 1965, just a year after I had moved from Hertz. So I had the benefit of working in effect within the ITT organization, and exposure to what I still believe were the most remarkable management talents that the company had in that era. It also gave me exposure to the legendary Harold Geneen at his monthly review meetings, either in Brussels or New York. I learnt a lot about management while we were owned by ITT. I guess Geneen became a mentor, as had a man called Donald Petrie, who was responsible for me joining the Hertz organization as a management trainee in the first place, and encouraged me to emigrate to the United States in 1958. He also was responsible for my moving from the Hertz organization to Avis. We are still very close friends, and I see him often.

Looking back, I suppose my principle management triumph was the successful privatization of British Airways, with very good Stock Market quotations in London and New York simultaneously. It was very time-consuming: apart from anything else, we had to settle the infamous Laker lawsuit, which involved, as I recall, something like 12 other defendants, almost all of whom were in other countries. Quite clearly the Government was not going to privatize British Airways until that lawsuit was out of the way, so we had to take it upon ourselves to get all of the other defendants to agree on settlement terms, as well as Laker and the people acting on his behalf. And that delayed our privatization.

I don't know in an overall sense what image people have of me. Obviously I read most of the comments that appear in the media, but there's not much consistency about them. People talk of me as being a good manager, and I can hardly disapprove of that. My greatest strengths are my international experience over the many years, and hopefully the leadership and direction I am able to bring to an organization. I think I'm a good people picker, though I have made mistakes, but in the businesses I've headed up over the years we have managed to get some good teams together.

Frankly, anybody who says they don't make mistakes has to be a liar, because everybody makes mistakes from time to time. The critical thing in business is to have an organization structure and a management team that is able to recognize when somebody has made a mistake, and hopefully act on it and correct it as quickly as possible. That's why you have organization structures, and why you have different levels of approval for capital expenditures and other major commitments.

In the event of a crisis, you need to approach it with a cool head while endeavouring to assess what the facts are. Sometimes you have to do this very quickly indeed, at the same time providing as much leadership and direction as you possibly can according to your level of responsibility. Getting people to bring you the bad news is one of the more difficult aspects, particularly for senior management and senior executives. The only way I think you can try to overcome that is by not reacting badly if somebody does bring you bad news. Try to absorb it, and to respond perhaps when you've cooled off. A heated reaction will almost certainly destroy any prospect of good communication upward in the organization.

Non-executive directors are very important indeed; they bring a balance to the perspective of the board's deliberations. It is terribly easy for executive directors to get a very biased viewpoint, a very introverted one. It's absolutely essential to have strong non-executive directors who are able to bring that better balance. And they have clear responsibilities; among them, certainly, to ensure the succession on the executive management side.

Everybody has weaknesses. It's very difficult for the individuals themselves to name those weaknesses – it's usually easier to get other people to pinpoint them – but from my standpoint, I suppose perhaps one of my weaknesses is the level of detail that I get into. I defend that on the basis that I think detail is what a service business is all about, therefore it is wise and sensible for a chief executive to get into the details from time to time. But I do recognize that I can be criticized for the extent to which I do it. And I expect my wife would say my failure to ever manage to get any reasonable period of holiday is a weakness. In the last three years I've wound up with it being at least partially demolished.

I'm not sure that it's necessarily the role as chief executive that I like. You have to tie it in to the particular business that you're in, because there are horses for courses. I have spent almost all of my working life in the service businesses, very heavily in the international arena, and I really have enjoyed all of the jobs I've had at whatever level. Generally speaking, I've also enjoyed working with all of my colleagues, so I have overall quite a warm feeling about all that I have done. I suppose there are the odd things that I might have done differently with the benefit of hindsight, but that's inevitable.

There's nothing I really dislike about my role, except sometimes I wish I had a bit more time for myself; for my personal and family life. The only thing I regret was that I never really saw my daughter grow up. I was travelling so much over those years; before I realized it she was at university and off and gone. But I think a stable family life is a very important contributor to being able to do your job well.

For relaxation, I work. I like cross-country skiing, but I don't very often have the opportunity to do it. Tennis is my principle sport, and I think it does help you to have a healthy attitude towards work. I'm only sorry I don't get as much chance to play as I would like. When I lived in the United States I used to play every week. But I do believe that as we move more and more into this global market-place – whatever business you're in – the pressures are just going to go on increasing, and the demands on one's time are just going to go on increasing. So I do worry occasionally about the general managers of the future, and how we are really going to be able to bring them on and develop them with the wide-ranging experience that I believe is important to the top leaders of industry.

## TIPS FOR SUCCESS

- The application of common sense is extremely important indeed.

- Be a good communicator, and when I say communicator, I mean listener, as well as talker and director.

- At a senior level, you've got to be certain that you're paying attention to your stakeholders' requirements. You've certainly got to deliver leadership if you're in a management position.

- You've got to be sure that you have a defined and understood strategy for your company, for your function, for your department. Then it's back to the communication thing; it's important that they know.

- You've also got to have vision. If you really want to succeed, you've got to be thinking about the future all the time.

- And on a very individual basis, the Boy Scouts' motto is a very appropriate one: be prepared. So many people go into a meeting without giving it any forethought. They are not prepared. This is where confusion arises and so much time gets wasted.

# 12

# Brian Pitman

*Chief Executive, Lloyds Bank*

*Brian Pitman has been Chief Executive of Lloyds Bank since 1983. He has spent most of his career with Lloyds, and has a wide range of experience in domestic and international banking, including spells in Europe and the US. In 1976 he was appointed an Executive Director of Lloyds Bank International, responsible for the UK and Asia-Pacific divisions, and became Deputy Chief Executive in 1978. Four years later he was appointed Deputy Chief Executive of the Lloyds Bank Group. He is a Director of Lloyds Bank plc, The National Bank of New Zealand and NBNZ Holdings, and Chairman of Lloyds First Western Corporation.*

The essence of coping with the future is anticipation. If you can reach an accurate judgement about what is going on in the world, and what is likely to happen over the next few years, then you will cope better than somebody who is suddenly surprised by events.

We called the recession quite early, and we weren't wrong in our judgement. There was a lot of discussion at that time about hard landings, soft landings, medium-soft landings and so on, but we decided back in May 1989 that we were in for a big one. I remember it well. We then had to convince our staff that we were in for a recession, because this would change their behaviour. We also had to convince our customers; we were trying to prepare them for a rough time. We wanted them to take steps there and then in order to cope with the downturn. Unfortunately, it's not the kind of news people want to receive. They want to hear that it will be wonderful tomorrow and the sun will shine. If you say 'Be prepared. It's getting very cloudy and we're in for some tremendous storms,' they don't want to know.

But the first step was to try to persuade the managers and staff, and that took some months. They didn't want to believe it; they thought we were being pessimistic. After all, the bank had been enjoying an extremely prosperous period. But we knew the UK could not possibly sustain that rate of economic growth, and we could see interest rates beginning to climb in different parts of the world. We were already seeing very serious effects of recession in New Zealand, Australia and, to some extent, the US, so it was only a matter of time before it came here. The fact that it took some months to convince our own people delayed action. If we could have done it the following day, their behaviour would have changed immediately, but you can't do it that quickly in an organization this big.

What made this recession different is the extent to which the services industry was hit. Heavy industrial areas have experienced many recessions over the centuries, but to some parts of Britain it was completely new. If you have never been used to any level of unemployment, even 3 per cent seems high. Whereas those areas which have suffered recession involving 15 per cent unemployment in the past have learned to cope with it. So there were two big differences. First of all, it hit the service industries, not just the financial service industries, but the whole of the service industries. It has also been very much a white collar recession.

In addition, it affected the US, Canada, Australia, New Zealand, Britain and other Anglo Saxon countries more or less at the same time. It's the English-speaking countries' disease, partly because of business philosophy, and partly because we are all very much market economies. To some extent, we are still adjusting to the full effect of free markets. Deregulation has also played a part, so it has been a combination of factors. In many industries, deregulation has shown up serious excess capacity.

In retrospect, we wish we had anticipated the recession even earlier. Had we anticipated it in 1988 we would have taken action that much earlier, but in boom years, people tend to be over-confident. So in banks all around the world, you had over-confident borrowers meeting over-confident lenders, and that leads to a lot of bad loans. In some parts of Lloyds we have been hit by this recession harder than ever before. The level of provisions on personal borrowing was higher than we've ever seen, and from different categories of customers. Unemployment in the white collar industries has been higher, and some of these people were very heavily committed. The Big Bang was also an important factor. A lot of people, sometimes very young, had very high salaries during the period of Big Bang. They didn't dream they would lose their jobs, but they have.

We have had substantial reductions in the number of staff

at Lloyds, but one of our objectives was to avoid compulsory redundancy, so wherever possible we encouraged early retirement or voluntary severance. We reduced the number of staff by 8,000 from a total workforce of 75,000 in about 1991, but only a tiny number were compulsory redundancies.

One thing we didn't anticipate was the invasion of Kuwait. That had a dramatic effect upon the world. We were already well into the recession, and it was made worse by the Gulf War because the whole of the leisure industry was dramatically affected. Flights, holidays and international conferences were cancelled. A lot of our customers are in the leisure business, and in some cases their sales dropped by 90 per cent. All of their expectations and plans based around cash flows were changed. There was a tremendous downturn as a result of the Gulf War that we certainly didn't predict. January and February of 1991 was one of the lowest points for activity in the world. It was a time of tremendous uncertainty for so many people, and when people are uncertain they don't do anything. They tend to sit at home. In the case of the Gulf War, they sat at home and watched the television. They didn't go to restaurants, hotels had virtually no bookings . . . and all these people are our customers. Banks only do well when their customers do well. When customers do badly, so do the banks.

Many shallow-rooted companies which were formed in the second half of the 1980s just hadn't got enough strength to survive the kind of downturn we experienced. I think there was a belief among some people that we had conquered the old business cycle. They thought we were now going to be able to continue with more and more growth, and that it would go on for ever. Others were talking about soft landings; they were predicting, at worst, a shallow recession. Even now, some people would say that in terms of declining GDP, this recession has not been enormous. But for certain segments of industry, it's been the biggest I have ever known. Certainly for a lot of the service industries, which didn't exist before. Again, it was a question of excess capacity combined with the recession. A lot of businesses were doing very well in the boom years. It was an amazing period for ideas and creativity as more and more people joined the bandwagon and invented new services to meet new needs

Of course, when service companies go bust, banks haven't got much to fall back on. There's not much to recover out of the assets. Take video shops, for example. If the demand for videos goes down because people are hard up, there isn't a queue of people waiting to buy second-hand video tapes when the shop goes bust. So the level of bad debts has been very high indeed. The banks are definitely partly to blame, there's no question of that. It was a time of expansion when the banks were backing a tremendous number of new people on the assumption that this growth would indeed continue.

With hindsight, the banks should have been more cautious. They would have lost a lot of business, of course, but this is one of the great difficulties of banking. If you are running a bank in a fairly small town – say 20,000 people – and you are constantly saying 'No', word gets around remarkably quickly. You become known as the 'Abominable No Man', and customers won't bother to come and see you.

Even now, the percentage of bad debts in relation to the whole is small. But you've got to get such a high percentage right to make a satisfactory return. Some businesses might find a 5 per cent rate of bad debts acceptable, whereas for a bank it would be a colossal amount of money to lose. Some banks have only got 5 per cent of capital to their loans. If they're then going to make losses of 5 per cent, the capital has gone.

One of the root causes is that there was serious excess capacity in financial services businesses all over the world. In the 1970s and 1980s, many people decided it was the growth industry. Well, what happened – as is very common in business – is that too many people put their money into financial services. Too many people diversified, so you had too much capital chasing too few opportunities. And when that happens, the banks are driven to compete on both price and risk. First they reduce their prices to attract more customers, then, when they find they still aren't getting a high enough share, they increase the amount of risk they are willing to take.

For example, we as a bank have always been pretty cautious on mortgage lending. By that I mean we have never been willing to grant a very high percentage of the purchase price, nor have we been willing to grant a very high multiple of salary. Others, in order to compete, offered a higher percentage or a higher multiple of salary. So we couldn't be surprised if a lot of people borrowed money from them rather than us. It means, as an organization, that you lose market share, and it's probably the most sensible thing you ever do. But your employees do not like it, because they don't like saying no to the customers. When I talk to other bankers around the world, it's a similar story. A competitor offers to lend one of your customers the money at half a per cent less, and without any security. Your branch manager is then faced with the prospect of losing the customer or matching the terms. So often, the manager, quite naturally, will want to match the terms. He will not want to lose the customer; it's a very difficult judgement for him. And all the banks in the world have suffered as a result.

Of course, hell hath no wrath like a man or woman who owes you money and can't pay it back. It's very difficult to make people like that happy. The answer is, we shouldn't have lent them as much money. We should have actually said to them at the time 'This is not in your interests.' If we couldn't convince them, and they threatened to go across the road to another bank, we should have let them. We should definitely have been more disciplined with the customers. They might not have liked it, but they'd be thanking us now.

As we come out of this recession, the banks are bound to be more cautious. And I think they will tend to go back to lending for working needs, rather than providing quasi-equity. Most banks have gone too far in providing the stake which ought to have been the proprietor's. The balance between how much the bank provides and how much the proprietor provides was out of kilter for a time. We're now seeing a reversal of that process, which will be healthy for banks and customers alike. And in future, I think more time will be spent on giving advice before the money is lent, so people can see the pitfalls. Banks will get more involved in business plans in order to help customers find realistic solutions.

After this period of tremendous turbulence, I'm quite optimistic that we could move into a period of greater stability overall. We have learned the lesson, at least for the time being, that high inflation doesn't pay. It doesn't pay entrepreneurs, it doesn't pay pensioners or employees. Now people can see that high inflation and a boom and bust cycle is not good for anybody, they will be willing to change their behaviour. So we have a very good prospect of economic growth, unaccompanied by high inflation.

One big lesson to learn is that in order to protect yourself, you need to tuck away enough money during the good years to take care of the bad. Remember the song *Let The Good Times Roll*? Well, be quite persuaded that the good times will not roll for ever. But what does it mean, tucking money away in the good times? It means actually reducing your consumption. The American expression 'Having it all' seems to have fallen into decline, but the dream was that you could have the best of everything at 25 years old. Well, you probably can't. At 25, you need to be tucking enough away for when you're 30. And if you're a company, just because you've had a fantastic three years doesn't mean the next three years will be just as good. You have to put money aside.

But it sounds like preaching when you give this sort of message to people. They'll take it during a recession, but when the good times roll again, they find it very difficult to curb themselves. 'Why shouldn't I buy that extra company? I'm having a very successful time' they say, but it all comes back to liquidity. Liquidity is absolutely essential. At the very least, you need to have something you can turn into liquidity. If you are a small businessman and you have a terrific year, you might go out and buy yourself an expensive motor car. But if the next year is a bad one, don't think you can convert this expensive motor car into liquidity. You'll probably wind up selling it at a loss. It's very difficult to persuade people of the importance of liquidity.

One of the great things about real terms of interest – in other words, interest rates above the rate of inflation – is that the saver has something to gain. We've had real rates of interest for some years now, which means depositors have got a positive return. As a result, the savings ratio has increased substantially. If you create more savings, you ought to be able to create more investment. And if you make property a less attractive investment – which is what has happened – then that money can be used to invest in manufacturing and other industries. It's easy to see how we could get ourselves into a so-called virtuous circle. If we can control inflation and get investment going into industry instead of speculative ventures, we'll be much more successful as a country.

It wasn't just the Conservative Government that used high interest rates to control inflation: it was an international phenomenon. We can't insulate ourselves from what's going on in the rest of the world. If the Deutschmark or Yen interest rate goes up tomorrow, the pound will be affected. If you said 'Well, the rest of them can have high interest rates, but we're not going to', the decline in the pound would be inevitable. We live in an international, interdependent world, and we tend to get dragged up and down together. There is much greater convergence, not just in interest rates, but in time. The actual time that these recessions and booms take place . . . we feed off one another. And the effect of communication technology all around the world has been dramatic. When a worldwide television station makes an announcement, information passes amazingly quickly and people take notice. If something is going on in the United

States, whether you're in Britain or France, you're going to be affected. So the days when we could have a totally different interest rate in Britain are long gone. We're influenced by the interest rates in other countries, and by their prosperity or decline.

One of the healthiest aspects of the whole process of internationalization and deregulation is increased competition. It sharpens up businesses and gives people more choice. If customers think they can get a better deal from a French or German bank, they will go to them instead. It's a fundamental change in financial services that people shop around until they get what they want. It means we'll have to keep on our toes. These days lots of people come to us wanting to buy property abroad. They want to know about finance, tax advice, legal advice and so on. We've had to equip ourselves to deal with that. We've made special arrangements with other European banks to provide the service. Our customers don't regard it as essential that we do everything ourselves; as long as we can tell them how to get the service, or provide it through an intermediary, they're happy.

You can only survive if you're competitive. You've got to persuade people to buy from you rather than somebody else. This means that companies have to adapt again and again to the customers' needs, whereas up until now there's been a great tendency for companies to believe that customers have to adapt to them. I think we'll see a very big improvement in productivity as people pay attention to the basics in order to reduce the cost per unit. And the moderation of wage demands is already happening, which is very beneficial. Employees can see that while excessive pay increases are all right in the short term, in the longer term, if the company goes bust, it's not much good for a career. One of the challenges for management is to get everybody to understand that stability is better for them, because in real terms they will be making better progress. Switzerland and Germany have enjoyed this sort of economic growth for years, with low inflation and great improvements in standards of living. And that's what we have a good chance of doing now.

In some ways, the great disadvantage of globalization is a 'sameness'. I don't like the fact that all these cities which were so different have become more and more the same. I remember Bangkok as this wonderful, mysterious city of the East. Now it has a whole host of international hotels to serve me, just as if I was in New York or London. It has the same traffic problems, and even the joy of being able to see totally different fashions has gone. Countries, capitals, cities and towns are becoming more and more the same. And the more similar we become, the less creative people get. The originality has gone.

But overall, the benefits of globalization are enormous. The fact that you can now get on a plane from London and fly directly to Tokyo is a tremendous advantage. That alone gives me seven days extra a year. Plastic cards can be used in machines all over Europe; this is an enormous change. And while we may regret never being able to escape from the dreaded fax machine, the use of it in different parts of the world makes life so much easier. The speed of communication, therefore the speed of response and the speed of service, is being transformed by technology, and I don't think we've scratched the surface of it yet. The opportunities for improving standards of living because of technology are huge, and I think the future is going to be very exciting.

As long as you can keep up with the game, and preferably ahead of it, then you should be successful. Being international as an individual is an increasingly necessary quality for a manager. You learn so much from other countries. The turning point in my career came when I was sent to Europe on a year's training to learn how different businesses were run. I spent another year in the United States looking at different ways of managing financial services, and it had a dramatic effect on me. It opened my eyes and taught me that there are many ways of skinning a cat. The man who runs UK retail banking for us had all his training in Brazil, and he's a real change agent. He doesn't say 'This is the way we've always done it, therefore this is the way we are always going to do it.' He says, 'Here are some alternatives; this might be a better way.' People of different nationalities come up with different ideas, and that is very healthy.

If you want to be successful, you've got to be the best. The best for customers, the best for employees and the best for shareholders. To be a successful manager, the ability to manage people is the most important quality of the lot. One of the tendencies of the last few years has been to move away from the management of people towards deal-making jobs. You get great satisfaction out of cutting a deal, whether it's selling a house or buying a company. The adrenalin flows, and it is a very exciting environment in which to operate. But a much more difficult task is managing a group of people to deliver goods to the consumer in the way that they want them delivered, at a price they want to pay. That is the real skill of management, because you're trying to motivate one group of people – the employees – to satisfy another group of people – the customers – ultimately in order to earn a satisfactory return to the shareholders. There used to be a view that these things were all in conflict, but in my opinion, they're not. You cannot deliver value to the shareholders unless you deliver value to the customers.

Management in the 1990s is less autocratic than it was in the 1980s. The era of the autocratic manager is over. Even the days of what I call paternalistic management – 'Work hard, be a good boy and we'll look after you' – are numbered. The key to it is participation. The people closest to the customers have often got the best solutions. If we ask the people in our branches about the best way of serving our customers, they often have a better answer than any boffin sitting in head office. One of the challenges for me as chief executive of an organization with about 70,000 people working in different parts of the world is how to get the message from those people undiluted to me. And how to get the message I am trying to convey undiluted to them. That is one of the great challenges of management.

There is absolutely no substitute for face-to-face communication. The other day I was talking to a group of 50 people. We hired a little cinema with a tiered arrangement. These were not people in management, they were the people who really matter; the ones who serve the customers. We had a two-hour question-and-answer session. I learned a lot from them, and I think they learned something from me. It was real communication. The problem is how to communicate with a large number of people. We've tried videos, we've tried letters, but it's nothing like as effective as face-to-face communication. It's an absolutely endless task, but it's the most important one you undertake.

Sometimes the staff thank me for going to their particular branch, and I say 'Don't thank me, this is the business I am in. I want to understand how we're getting on with the customers. What are the problems here that I can do something about?' I'm not somebody from an ivory tower who suddenly appears claiming to know all the answers. People at the top of organizations do not know all the answers. But the people working with the customers frequently know the answers better than you, so if you can get the communication right, you can do something about the problems to make life easier for them. Real communication is the challenge. After all, if we could have conveyed the message more quickly in 1989 that we were going to have a recession, we would have been more effective.

Now, of course, the reverse is happening. I'm having to say 'Recessions do come to an end.' It's very interesting to see how young people who have been living in recessionary conditions for two or three years have reacted. Just as they believed the boom would never come to an end, they think we're going to be in recession for another five or six years. My view is that we're close to the bottom already, but there's a lag in time during which people believe these rotten conditions are going to go on for ever. They get terribly gloomy, and you have to try and lift them out of it.

One of the most common management mistakes is not being candid. I find that you can tell our people all sorts of bad news. You can say quite openly that times are going to be tough, there are going to be fewer jobs, fewer opportunities, and they will take it all. What they can't take is any kind of dishonesty. If you don't tell them what's going on, they're uncertain. It's much better to say 'There will be job reductions, but we're going to do our utmost to avoid compulsory redundancies'.

For example, in 1991 we settled at a rate of pay increase which was less than the other banks. That was difficult for our employees to understand. We are a successful bank, our results are among the best, so they wanted to know why they were getting a 5 per cent increase when the other banks were getting 7. The answer was that every extra 1 per cent more we gave would cost 650 jobs. And we, as responsible management, did not want to see 650 more jobs going because we knew the pain it would cause. The staff could understand that message. Nobody liked it – I couldn't make them happy about it – but if you're open and honest, they accept it. They could see that what we were doing was sensible. And I believe everybody in this organization will benefit as a result of our actions, because we're stronger and fitter than we would otherwise have been.

The great satisfaction with this job is trying to keep the business right at the top of the first division. We've done extremely well as a bank, but it's like being at the top of any sporting league: the challenge is how to stay there. I get real satisfaction from working in a team of different people with a variety of talents. I'm surrounded by stimulating people with creative brains, new ideas and a sense of humour; it's fun to be with them. What I miss most is being separated from the customers. It happened the day I moved from being the manager of Threadneedle Street to being a general manager. Even though Threadneedle Street is a very big outfit in financial terms, you're still in touch every minute with the sharp end of the business.

And that is a great challenge for me now; how to stay in touch. In an organization as big as ours, if you're not careful, you get detached. But I visit a lot of branches and I meet people all the time to know what's going on.

We've been quite good at anticipating what would happen in the industry, and because we have been able to persuade our people that our assumptions about the future are pretty sound, we've been able to change faster than the competition. Anticipation and preparing for structural change have been key ingredients in our success. And I think we have managed to introduce into this organization a culture which is about creating value for shareholders by creating value for customers. In the last ten years, we've certainly shifted very substantially towards a belief that it is the ultimate test of success. So we've been able to change some of the basic philosophies in this organization, and that has been very satisfying. Meanwhile, we've been successful at a lot of ventures, which gives everybody pleasure. But there's nothing like seeing our young people growing into really outstanding individuals; that is one of the most satisfying aspects of all.

Of course, every man on earth has learned from mistakes he would prefer not to have made. I've got no time for people who say if they could have their time all over again they'd do exactly the same, because if you could, then you wouldn't make those mistakes. I made the mistake of buying a bank in Canada which we then had to sell. We misjudged the acquisition; what we got was not what we thought we were going to get. It also taught me a real lesson about the need to understand the culture of an organization before you make an acquisition. The financial figures can be good, but the culture is also important. That's the main reason why we didn't buy a securities house. We believed it would be very difficult to combine the culture of a securities house with the culture of a commercial bank.

I tend to define culture as 'the way things are done around here'. Having played a lot of different sports in my life, I notice it with teams. One will be absolutely dedicated to winning the match, while another just wants to go and play cricket on a Saturday afternoon, have a good time and a few drinks afterwards. They play together, but they have a totally different culture. Giving up cricket is one of my great regrets, but you get to a point where you should hang up your boots. These days I play golf in my spare time. I'm a regular theatregoer, I'm very keen on music and I see a lot of friends.

Family life provides a tremendous haven. Having children certainly keeps you right down to earth at all times. You can have two separate lives to some extent. One of them can be a complete escape from business. You do need to escape; it helps you stay objective. If you don't, you can lose the woods from the trees. You've got to get the balance right so the little things don't get on top of you, because that would be the great danger for a chief executive. Many, many things go wrong when you're the chief executive of a bank. People come in and say 'Brian, I'm sorry, but we've just lost 20 million dollars on this deal.' There's no point blowing your top, because it's going to happen again and again in an organization this big. And if you don't have a sense of proportion, you won't be a very good leader.

I'm not on any other board of directors due to lack of time. It's probably good to cram in one non-executive directorship if you can, because again, you see how other people skin the cat. I regard our non-executive directors at Lloyds as the best, and probably the cheapest, consultants in the business. Certainly they are the best possible value for money. They are extremely experienced at running other businesses and often have already been down the paths that we are about to take, therefore they can offer the most outstanding advice.

I thoroughly enjoy my job. People are always surprised when they come into banking by how many different challenges there are. They think it's going to be dull and dreary, but in an organization like this, you have the lot. You have every kind of individual imaginable, and that's what makes it so fascinating.

## TIPS FOR SUCCESS

- Do your present job as well as you possibly can, because that will give you the best chance of getting the next one.

- Try to see the wider picture while you're quite young. I worked under the general managers while I was a young man, so I got very close to the top of the organization. I didn't have the power, but I could see what was happening, so I knew what this job entailed many years ago. It was a great advantage to be able to see the wider picture.

- Always concentrate on trying to improve your skill at managing people. If you can't lead people, if you can't inspire them and give them clear goals, you're not likely to be very successful.

- You've got to get down to details. If all you're looking for is the grand design, then you won't be as successful as somebody who really understands the details.

- It is absolutely crucial to have a sense of humour, because it's the only thing that will keep you afloat when you hit the rocks. A sense of humour is vital to success.

# 13

# Sir Robert Scholey

*Chairman, British Steel*

*Sir Robert Scholey is Chairman of British Steel. Born in 1921, he took a degree at Sheffield University before serving in the Royal Electrical and Mechanical Engineers from 1943 to 1947, where he attained the rank of Captain. Sir Robert has spent the whole of his working life in the steel industry. He joined Steel Peech and Tozer at Rotherham as an engineer, and before the industry was nationalized worked for the United Steel Companies. In 1972 he moved to British Steel's head office in London, and became Chief Executive the following year. In 1976 he was appointed Deputy Chairman, and in 1986 became Chairman. He is a Non-Executive Director of Eurotunnel and is on the National Health Service Policy Board.*

The worldwide depression of the steel market started with *perestroika* and Tiananmen Square, when the big producers of steel found themselves shut out of both the Russian and Chinese markets. It was made worse by the fact that the the US economy had also slowed down, and as a result, steel prices are weak all over the world. This depression has gone on for longer than we expected, and we are not in step with the Government's prognostications of an upturn in the UK economy. We believe the steel industry will continue to be depressed for most of 1992.

A recession does, of course, present an opportunity to reduce your costs and reshape your organization better than at any other time. Your people understand the changes you are making; they don't like them, but they know they are necessary, and therefore you are able to get on with it. If you don't, you are being foolish, because when the upturn does come, you won't emerge from this slack period with improved cost performance and improved management. So we did what we could to improve our cost structures at the earliest opportunity. We've had to wind down our operations in Scotland because we needed to reduce our manufacturing costs, so the more we make on fewer sites, the better. British Steel has been in battle for years now, and if we don't know what to do in a crisis, nobody does. We have a history of knowing how to crash-diet, and we would never over-expose ourselves to financial risk. We're pretty well debt free, and as a matter of policy we would not allow our gearing to rise to anywhere near the levels of our competitors.

High pay can be properly structured to give low costs, but obviously there can be an employment factor involved. Capital-intensive industry cannot be used as a means of accommodating surplus labour. Every government is aware of the dangers of high unemployment because it goes hand in hand with electoral unpopularity, but the reality is that it will take time for manufacturing industry to make itself more efficient and generate the cash for new investment which in turn will create new jobs. And no government is able to stay in power long enough for that to happen.

I don't believe that nationally we can satisfy the needs of the country on service industries alone, and the manufacturing base in Britain is certainly too weak. Although I am an admirer of Margaret Thatcher, she was very *laissez-faire* as far as the manufacturing industry was concerned, which in my view was incorrect. The Government needs to be more involved. I don't mean we should go back to handing State money out, but there is a need for the Department of Trade and Industry to be taken more seriously. The Secretary of State should be a senior, and he should be known to be important within the Cabinet. His role could be to examine the various industrial sectors of the economy.

He's got plenty of civil servants to help him discover where they're failing in the balance of trade, where they're poorly managed, and where interest rates really are affecting them badly. There is need to examine carefully why our entrepreneurial abilities seem to be so diminished. Clearly, if you look around Britain today, you will see some enterprises which are internationally competitive, but there are too few of them. Why are there so few? Are we producing sufficient graduates for industry? And if graduates don't want to go into industry, why is this? All these questions need to be answered.

In the second half of the 1980s, money was growing in value year on year. You could buy a company expecting it to be worth x per cent more the following year, so it was obviously a high inflationary period, not just in the money sense, but in people's appetite for adventure. They thought the balloon was going to go up and up, ascending like a lark into the sky, and that was a mistake. The economy has never been like that, and it never will be. You have always to spare a thought for what will happen when the balloon stops going up. As a private individual, you either have something in the bank for a rainy day, or you don't. If you don't, and you live to the hilt, then, when the rainy day comes, you are in trouble. The climate of the country should not encourage people to live to the hilt by extending easy credit. I certainly believe that credit was made too freely available, and as a result, many companies ran into difficulties because they over stretched themselves. Many of them over-diversified, which was a mistake. Even if you're good at what you do, have you any reason to believe you might be good at something you haven't traditionally been involved with?

Everybody likes to formulate corporate strategies; it can almost become a secondary industry, if you're not careful. But clearly, every company needs a strategic route forward. You need a very good understanding of the market you're in, and of technological advances. You also need to ensure that your management resource is going to be adequate to achieve your objective. And you must make sure that the cash requirements of your strategy are realistic. There's no point in dreaming up a project that's going to cost money you haven't got a cat in hell's chance of generating.

British Steel has never diversified; we have stuck to what we know best. We are totally international, and we are gearing ourselves for a high productivity economy. Our strategy is to grow in North America and West Germany, but we are not planning to increase our capacity in the UK. You have to recognize that the world is getting smaller, and we're living in a time when free trading is the vogue. That is going to increase, because it is clear that free trading gently lifts standards of living. Everybody will benefit from globalization; for example, we shall be supplying the Japanese plants when they arrive here.

Generally, I think the British are ignorant about the EC. British Steel has been in Europe since before the treaty was signed. I'm totally for the free market: get rid of the tariff barriers, have standard forms of accountancy, no State aid in the Union, and so on. But I'm against political union. We've seen the homogeneity of the USSR being blown apart at the same time as the European Parliament is wanting to bring disparate people together, and I don't believe it will work.

At a dinner party recently I reminded the guests of somebody we all knew who used to say 'You achieve in life no more than those who work for you deliver for you.' To me, management is what it always was, and will always be. A successful manager is one who creates a climate in which employees can deliver their best; that's what he's there for. At the same time, he has to know what his customers want, and give it to them. He also has to make sure that the prices will generate an appropriate return on the sale to help refurbish the business. On the whole, customer service is not very good in this country. When you walk into a shop to buy something, you get the feeling they're not really bothered whether they sell it to you or not. Even in a restaurant, people don't care whether they give you a good meal. I think it's rather sad. It's always nice when you feel you are actually being sold something by a person who really wants to please you. There is too much sloppiness in our national persona. What we need is to take pride in service.

How you treat people is very important. Some managers distance themselves from those who work for them, and I think that is wrong. You have to have some flexibility in the relationship, and you must pick people who understand that there are times when you can be close to them, but there are also times when you will have to stand back. There are no barriers between me and my employees; I can relate to anyone. The ability to pick the right people is very important, though I have made mistakes. I certainly wouldn't pick anybody just because of his CV; it's the track record that counts. It's a bit like horse-racing; you put your money on a horse with a track record, so you put your money on people with a track record too. Then you have to observe their performance, and see whether you like their style. Notice how they express themselves when you ask about what they are doing. Are they concise and to the point? You also need to get a feel for how they treat others who work for them.

Leadership is not everybody's gift. We are what we are, and after all, not everybody wants to lead. And we do have to have followers. I think I am a a good leader – a good captain – and generally I've been successful in picking good lieutenants. I think I have managed to create a climate in which people can do their best, which is a strength. I know the steel industry very well, and I have developed a very international outlook. I have broadened my personal background from just being an engineer, and I can understand disciplines other than my own. But maybe at times I take too much control, and that can be a weakness. If somebody wants to do something which I'm not sure about, then I test it out very vigorously instead of just letting him go ahead. It's important to strike a balance, so that you can spot the person who knows what he's talking about and trust him to get on with it, while being able to recognize the person who is a bit out of his depth.

My most fulfilling management achievement was bringing the company into the private sector. But my biggest mistake was believing that it was possible to persuade the unions to adopt the necessary changes to make the company viable without industrial dispute. I thought if we presented them with all the facts and figures, they would support us. Unfortunately, they didn't, and we had a massive great strike which nearly ruined everybody.

I suppose if I could have my time over again, I might do something else. I used to fancy the idea of being a surgeon; I think engineering of the human body would be a very worthwhile occupation. But I do enjoy my role as chairman of British Steel. How can you be a good boss if you don't enjoy what you do?

## TIPS FOR SUCCESS

- You have to be a good people picker. Don't go by their CVs; it's track record that counts.

- You have to be blessed with some charisma if people are to follow you. You've got to inspire confidence.

- All people like to feel they are being well-managed, so you need to be decisive. You have to know what you're talking about, what you're doing, and where you're going. You need a clear strategic route.

- Make sure the cash requirements for your strategy are realistic.

- Remember that your task is to create a climate in which people can deliver their best.

# Index